WHAT CHRISTIANITY IS
ALL ABOUT

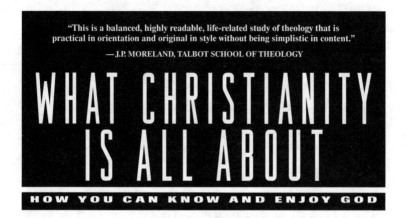

"This is a balanced, highly readable, life-related study of theology that is practical in orientation and original in style without being simplistic in content."

—J.P. MORELAND, TALBOT SCHOOL OF THEOLOGY

WHAT CHRISTIANITY IS ALL ABOUT

HOW YOU CAN KNOW AND ENJOY GOD

ALAN KENT SCHOLES

NAVPRESS

BRINGING TRUTH TO LIFE

P.O. Box 35001, Colorado Springs, Colorado 80935

The Navigators is an international Christian organization. Our mission is to reach, disciple, and equip people to know Christ and to make Him known through successive generations. We envision multitudes of diverse people in the United States and every other nation who have a passionate love for Christ, live a lifestyle of sharing Christ's love, and multiply spiritual laborers among those without Christ.

NavPress is the publishing ministry of The Navigators. NavPress publications help believers learn biblical truth and apply what they learn to their lives and ministries. Our mission is to stimulate spiritual formation among our readers.

© 1999 by Alan Scholes
Library of Congress Catalog Card Number: 98-55585
ISBN 1-57683-127-2

Some of the ideas contained in chapter one originally appeared in "Levels of Belief in the Pauline Epistles: A Paradigm for Evangelical Unity" by Alan K. Scholes and Stephen M. Clinton, *Bulletin of the Evangelical Philosophical Society* 1991. Vol. 14, No. 2, 70-84. Used by permission.

Cover image by Superstock
Image manipulation by Steve Eames

Some of the anecdotal illustrations in this book are true to life and are included with the permission of the persons involved. All other illustrations are composites of real situations, and any resemblance to people living or dead is coincidental.

Unless otherwise identified, all Scripture quotations in this publication are taken from the *New American Standard Bible* (NASB), © The Lockman Foundation 1960, 1962, 1963, 1968, 1971, 1972, 1973, 1975, 1977.

Scholes, Alan Kent, 1947-
    What Christianity is all about : how you can know and enjoy God / Alan Kent Scholes.
       p.   cm.
    ISBN 1-57683-127-2 (paper)
    1. Theology, Doctrinal.   I. Title.
BT77.S373   1999   98-55585
230—dc21   CIP

Printed in the United States of America

1 2 3 4 5 6 7 8 9 10 11 12 13 14 15 / 05 04 03 02 01 00 99

To my mother,
Murene Lucina Hubbard Scholes,
who first showed me,
through her life and words,
that God could be enjoyed
with both heart and mind.

CONTENTS

ACKNOWLEDGMENTS

Most books worth reading take a long time to reach print. The gestation of this work has been, perhaps, longer than most.

The story of *What Christianity Is All About* began in 1976 when Ted Martin invited me to teach a Doctrine Survey course at the Campus Crusade for Christ summer Institute of Biblical Studies. Thank you, Ted, for believing in me then, and continuing to believe in me through all the years since, as my mentor, professor, and seminary colleague. You have given selflessly right up to being willing to cover some of my class lectures so I could finish the manuscript!

By the mid-1970s, I had taught very little—and never in theology—so Ted sent me to David Sunde, who had originated the Doctrine Survey course in Campus Crusade. Thanks, Dave, for generously sharing your notes with me that summer, collaborating with me on the course for many years thereafter, and setting an example of how theology can be communicated with both intelligence and passion. No doubt many of your ideas (and your overall approach to learning about God) are reflected in these pages.

I first began to develop the paradigm of "convictions, persuasions, and opinions" under the guidance of Steve Clinton during my own seminary years in the early 1980s. Thank you, Steve, for your tough-minded and generous-hearted mentoring through so many years.

I also appreciate the counsel of Campus Crusade leaders John Rogers, Mark Rutter, and Jack Mattern for their encouragement to begin developing the book in the mid-1990s. What can I say to my longtime faithful friend and Doctrine Survey collaborator, Conrad Koch? You believed in this book from the beginning and even used the manuscript with your own students. Your thoughtful suggestions (and theirs) have improved it greatly.

I'm grateful to my friend and colleague J. P. Moreland, who first suggested NavPress to publish the book and recommended me to them. Thanks, Jay, for your encouragement and suggestions, especially during the crucial summer when I was struggling to complete the manuscript.

I am also grateful to my many students at the International School of Theology and in the Campus Crusade new staff courses, who gave helpful suggestions and corrections, particularly to Doctrine Survey student Brenda Bartelt for her thorough, detailed proofreading.

Kudos to the members of the Plot & Blot literary society: Ray Albrektson, Janet Grant, Gary Stanley, and Kirsten Wilson. You cheerfully endured and graciously edited multiple versions of many chapters over a several-year period. I'm particularly grateful to my longtime friend, fellow Plot & Blotter, and literary agent, Janet Kobobel Grant: without you, very simply, this book would never have come to be. Special thanks are due to my NavPress editors, Steve Webb, Gary Wilde, and Sue Geiman, especially for patiently enduring all my naïve questions and ideas.

Most of all, I want to thank my wife, Jan. You encouraged me when I was ready to give up, you cheerfully picked up the slack when I had to set everything else aside to finish, and you even proofread several versions of the manuscript. I love and appreciate you more than I can say.

—ALAN KENT SCHOLES

CHAPTER ONE

OUR APPROACH: CONVICTIONS, PERSUASIONS, AND OPINIONS

SHARON PEERED AT ME THROUGH LARGE OVAL GLASSES. "THIS really isn't theology you're teaching us, is it?"

I had to look closely to make sure she wasn't teasing. Sharon was in her early twenties. She had joined the staff of a large mission agency and was taking my basic theology course as part of her ministry preparation.

"Well," I said, groping for words, "why do you ask?"

"Because every day when I leave your class, my heart is so filled with God's love, I just want to sing. I'm actually enjoying all this doctrine stuff!"

ENJOYING THROUGH KNOWING

Enjoying "doctrine" and "theology"? Somehow these words sound stiff and dull. However, *doctrine* is just another word for teaching, and *theology* simply means knowledge of God. I've called this book *What Christianity Is All About: How You Can Know and Enjoy God* because I hope your experience will be a little like Sharon's. My prayer is that as you explore Christian theology—what Christians believe—you will increasingly experience the deep, rich joy reserved for those who truly know Him.

And knowing is a key to enjoying. When asked, "Which is the great commandment in the Law?" Jesus answered, "YOU SHALL LOVE THE LORD YOUR GOD WITH ALL YOUR HEART, AND WITH ALL YOUR SOUL, AND WITH ALL YOUR MIND."[1] To most modern Christians, loving God with all your heart and soul makes sense. But how can we love God with our minds? I think the answer is that we need to understand what God has said about who He is, who we are, and how we can have a relationship with Him. Of course, knowing (and enjoying) God involves more than simply knowing *about* Him and what He has said. However, I am convinced that we cannot truly know God without also knowing a good deal about Him.

Recently I was listening to a radio psychologist. A young woman called in asking what she should do about her live-in boyfriend, who had been gone for three days, leaving no message or note.

"How long have you known him?"

"About four months."

"And how long has he been living with you?"

"About three months."

"Have you called the place where he lived before?"

"I don't know where he lived; I never called him there."

"Have you tried calling his work?"

"I don't have that number either."

"Have you dropped by his work to see if anyone there knows anything?"

"I don't know where he works or even the name of the company."

"How about his friends? Have you tried calling them?"

"He never mentioned any other friends."

"What about his parents, can you call them?"

"He never spoke of them; I don't know where they live or even if they're alive."

The psychologist paused and then asked, in obvious consternation, "Where did you meet this guy?"

"In a bar. We always met at the same bar."

"And what did he say when you asked him about his family or his friends or his work?"

There was moment of silence before the caller quietly said, "I never asked."

"You never asked? You never asked! And you say you love this man?"

"Yes, I love him very much, and I'm worried about him."

"Listen, dear, I met my husband ten years ago at a party. In the first half-hour of conversation, I found out who his parents were and where they lived, what he studied in college, where he worked, and lots more. I knew more about him in thirty minutes than you've learned living with this guy for three months! How can you say you 'love' him? You know nothing about the man!"

I think the psychologist was right. How can we genuinely love someone we know little about? The more we know about God—who He is, what He values, what He says about things—the more we can truly begin to love Him with all our minds. That is the purpose of this book: to help you discover what God has said concerning the wide variety of subjects He has told us about in the Bible, and as a result, to experience a deeper love relationship with Him.

In each of the areas of theology that follow, you will find a brief sketch of a particular doctrine—an area of teaching that God has given to us about Himself, about ourselves, or about the world. In a few pages you can grasp the basic ideas of what the Bible teaches and what Christians believe in this area of theology. We'll look at what we believe, why we believe it, and how our beliefs can bring us into a more intimate and enjoyable relationship with our God. To begin, let's explore an idea that may surprise you: not everything we believe as Christians needs to be, or even should be, held as a strong conviction.

RECOGNIZING THE LEVELS OF BELIEF

The seed for approaching theology as I will in this book was planted in my heart and mind many years ago when I first read *Mere Christianity* by C. S. Lewis. As a young Christian still in college, I wondered why some believers argued over what seemed like trivial points of belief. I was puzzled as well by those who called themselves Christians but denied basic doctrines like the deity of Christ or the Trinity. I was like a starving man invited to a feast when I read in Lewis's introduction that he was going to present "an agreed, or common, or central, or 'mere' Christianity."[2] But I wondered, wouldn't this just be some insipid, worthless, lowest-common-denominator theology? As if anticipating my question, Lewis went on to say that the common core of Christian belief "turns out to be something not only positive but pungent; divided from all nonChristian beliefs by a chasm to which the worst divisions inside Christendom are not really comparable at all."[3] In the remainder of his book, Lewis established two categories of views: those that are a part of "mere" Christianity and those that are not.

You might be wondering, Isn't this kind of distinction unbiblical? Isn't everything in Scripture equally essential? Shouldn't believers, once they understand a passage, hold its truth as firmly as they hold to the truths of any other passage? In this sense shouldn't every teaching of Scripture be a part of "mere" Christianity?

The answer to each of these questions must be a firm no. The New Testament writers themselves held more than one category of belief. They held some beliefs as nonnegotiable for all Christians, others as matters of individual conscience on which believers could have diversity of understanding without disunity, and other beliefs as solely matters of personal preference or style.

Sadly, the conflict and division that characterized Christianity in Lewis's day is still with us. The need for restoring a unity, based on a distinction between what is central in the Christian faith and what is secondary, is as great as it was when Lewis wrote *Mere Christianity* more than a half-century ago.

One of the best ways to understand and appreciate the kinds of distinctions we need to make is to look at the writings of the apostle Paul. Some people think of Paul as always dogmatic and unyielding. It's true that the apostle who jumps off the pages of Acts and his many letters was a man of strong convictions and bold action. But that is one reason I find it so intriguing that Paul didn't hold all of his beliefs at the same level of importance. I think we find in Paul's letters at least three distinct levels of belief: convictions, persuasions, and opinions.

Level 1: Convictions

Even though Paul was often a man of peace and tolerance, he considered some issues so crucial and central to the faith that he was willing to risk dividing the body of Christ over them. Paul told us about one such issue in his letter to the Galatians.

The conflict had to do with Peter (also called Cephas), who was the acknowledged leader of the church in Jerusalem, the center of first-century Christianity. As a good Jew, Peter had grown up eating only the prescribed Jewish foods. After his vision from God,[4] apparently Peter relaxed those rigorous standards and ate Gentile foods, at least when eating with Christians who had been converted from a Gentile background. When some legalistic Jewish believers arrived from Jerusalem, Peter "began to withdraw and hold himself aloof, fearing the party of the circumcision."[5] But the problem didn't end there. When Peter stopped eating Gentile food, "the rest of the Jews joined him in hypocrisy, with the result that even Barnabas was carried away by their hypocrisy."[6] Finally Paul could stand it no longer and publicly confronted Peter. "But when I saw that they were not straightforward about the truth of the gospel, I said to Cephas in the presence of all, 'If you, being a Jew, live like the Gentiles and not like the Jews, how is it that you compel the Gentiles to live like Jews?'"[7]

The issue of eating or abstaining from nonkosher food was not, as it might first appear, the real crux of what Paul believed at a conviction level. We know this because he told us in Romans 14 that issues like this are best left to individual persuasion. A far more serious issue was at stake in Antioch.

Peter's behavior, whether intentional or not, was threatening the unity of the body of Christ and confusing the means of salvation. Peter's withdrawal from eating with the Gentiles challenged the "truth of the gospel" that Paul had been preaching. Specifically, Peter was tacitly denying the doctrine of salvation by grace through faith alone, as the apostle made clear in Galatians 2:16. Paul was willing to take a strong, public stand because the issue was essential to salvation. The conduct of Peter and the other Jews seemed "calculated to throw obscurity and doubt on the true gospel."[8] In this instance Paul was making a conviction-level stand, not yielding in subjection "for even an hour, so that the truth of the gospel might remain with you."[9] In other words, Paul was willing to stand and fight, even risking a public controversy, because Peter's behavior struck at the heart of the gospel message. Any compromise at this point would have been tantamount to a loss of the gospel itself!

In Galatians 2, then, Paul was acting from *convictions* about matters crucial to salvation. These were not simply *persuasions* about which the apostle, although certain he was right, could allow other believers to disagree. Rather, in these cases Paul was willing to risk the unity he had spent so much of his life building. His rationale for taking such a deep risk was that it concerned the very heart and truth of the gospel.[10]

Convictions for Paul were matters of belief in which the gospel itself was at stake. In these matters Paul was not "tolerant." Rather, he confronted those in error and was ready to break fellowship with them if they did not repent.

Likewise, I think we believers today should have some doctrinal truths that we hold at a conviction level. I believe we should have very few convictions, but we should be willing to die (or suffer ridicule) for them. Someone has said, "If you have nothing worth dying for, you may have nothing worth living for!" I hope and pray that, if I were given the choice to either deny Christ or die, I would have the courage and grace to choose death, as have so many Christians through the centuries.

I believe our convictions should be tied to subjects we have studied for ourselves. Secondhand convictions are dangerous, although many Christians harbor them. Do you really want to die for something you merely heard a pastor or radio preacher say a decade ago? Also, convictions should be restricted to concepts clearly taught in many passages of Scripture. And we should expect confirmation by church history with a general, though perhaps not perfect, consensus.

Remember, breaking fellowship with those who significantly disagree at the conviction level is not only legitimate but often essential.[11] Some examples of doctrines that I think deserve to be held at the conviction level are the Trinity, the deity of Christ, and salvation by grace through faith. We will look more closely at each of these convictions in later chapters.

Level 2: Persuasions

We find a second level of belief in Romans 14. In verse 5 Paul stated, "One man regards one day above another, another regards every day alike. Let each man be fully persuaded in his own mind." Notice that while each person was to be fully persuaded, Paul wasn't insisting on uniformity of view among "fully persuaded" believers. Each person can have his or her own belief yet remain in unity with believers who disagree.[12]

"Persuaded" is a strong term meaning "having a filled-in, settled belief."[13] Initially it might seem that Paul was speaking here of the strongest possible level of theological conviction. However, as his argument continues, it becomes clear that this "full persuasion" should not be used as a basis for dividing personal fellowship with other believers or even for thinking badly of them. Paul said we should not judge other Christians or hold them in contempt. Why? Because we will "all stand before the judgment seat of God."[14] Therefore, Paul concluded we should stop judging believers and instead "determine this— not to put an obstacle or a stumbling block in a brother's way."[15] For Paul it was possible to have a "full persuasion" concerning a matter of faith or practice and yet not feel the need to break personal fellowship with those in the body of Christ who strongly disagree.

Some might object that Paul had in mind matters of Christian behavior that are in themselves morally neutral and that these principles cannot necessarily be applied to doctrinal controversy. However, many commentators through church history have seen this as a general principle applying to doctrine as well as behavior. One example would be William Shedd, writing a century ago, who commented on verse 5, "This is the general principle of action, in reference to points not essential to salvation."[16] In this broader view, Shedd followed Luther[17] and Calvin.[18]

Paul was saying there are many issues on which an individual, mature believer may have a settled, full persuasion and yet not be justified in judging his or her fellow Christian. The principle he drew is larger than any single issue: "Who are you to judge the servant of another?"(verse 4). For Shedd the dividing line was that which is not essential for salvation. Martin Luther came to the same conclusion.[19] Luther believed that there were matters worth disputing and even those that warranted breaking Christian fellowship.[20]

These verses in Romans 14 show that Paul held some issues as persuasions about which Christians should have firm beliefs while accepting other believers who disagree. Following Shedd and Luther, I would also propose that the proper dividing line between theological persuasions and those doctrinal convictions that would warrant confrontation and a risk of division should be whether the beliefs in question are essential to salvation.[21]

Most Christians have a fair number of persuasions, and the number of our persuasions generally increases as we study. One likely consequence of reading this book is that you will emerge with some new persuasions. Persuasions should be subjects on which we have studied enough to develop a clear and informed view. Persuasions often don't deal with the main themes of Scripture yet generally should be confined to subjects about which the Bible speaks. We can feel free to argue for our persuasions, but we should respect and cooperate with those who disagree. Some examples of persuasions would be millennial views, the role of "tongues," and the age of the earth.

Level 3: Opinions

A final level of belief is found in Paul's treatment of marriage in 1 Corinthians 7. In dealing with the question of celibacy, he said, "This I say by way of concession, not of command. Yet I wish that all men were even as I myself am." As a single man who devoted all his time and energy to serving the Lord, Paul wished all were free to pursue God and ministry with such single-minded devotion. But clearly Paul did not think this is God's will for everyone, for he went on to say that "each man has his own gift from God, one in this manner, and another in that" (verses 7-8).

The Greek word for "wish" is *thelo,* which in this context expresses "desire" or "design."[22] The apostle used the word three other times in this chapter. In verse 36 he said a father may, if he wishes, allow his unwed daughter to marry. Clearly, this was not Paul's own first choice, but he was giving permission for each man to carry out his own preference. Again, in verse 39, Paul said a widow may marry whom she wishes. And in verse 32 he said, "I want *[thelo]* you to be free from concern." In each case Paul was using the word in the sense of an individual desire or personal preference. Therefore, *thelo* frequently carries the sense of a strictly personal or even hypothetical wish. So when Paul said, "I wish all were like me," he was expressing his opinion that the celibate state is best.

Perhaps an even clearer example of Paul expressing an opinion comes in 1 Corinthians 7:40. In advising the widow, he said, "In my opinion she is happier if she remains as she is; and I think I also have the Spirit of God." The word "opinion" here is translated from the Greek *gnoman* (from the verb *ginosko*, "to know"). Used this way, it could mean a "judgment" or "opinion." However, to interpret this word as "judgment" in the sense of authoritatively handing down a directive does not make sense in the context. Paul had just said that she was free to marry (verse 39), so this was not a command but simply a friendly opinion from Paul.[23]

Elsewhere in this passage, Paul did speak authoritatively. In verse 12 the apostle undoubtedly expected his directives to be literally obeyed for he concluded his discussion in verse 17 with "and thus I direct. . . ." In this verse we find no hint of a disclaimer, no room left for individual conscience. But verses 25 and 40 are quite different. Clearly, neither of these is in the nature of a universal directive, for each carries a disclaimer in a nearby verse.

A more somber use of *thelo* comes from the lips of Christ in Gethsemane. When Jesus prayed, "Let this cup pass from Me; yet not as I will *[thelo]*, but as Thou wilt," it was not His conviction or even His persuasion that the cup would pass. It was simply His human wish to avoid the suffering that was before Him.[24]

Opinions are beliefs, desires, or even wishes that may not be clearly taught in Scripture or that may legitimately differ for various believers. Opinions may even be our own pet theories or prejudices, which may or may not turn out to be true. We will have many opinions, and they will change fairly frequently. Opinions may be on subjects that we have not personally studied or on which the Bible is silent or ambiguous. In dealing with these things, we should speak tentatively or label our views as "my opinion" or as "speculation." Some examples of views that

If boundary statements were only written to clarify who is and who is not a true Christian, then it might make sense to include only conviction-level beliefs.[25] However, many doctrinal statements, especially in recent centuries, have been designed to capture the distinctives of a ministry or a particular group of Christians and therefore include a mixture of conviction-, persuasion-, and sometimes even opinion-level beliefs.[26]

I think it's fine, and often a necessary protection, for a church or other Christian organization to require its leaders and teachers to adhere not only to those beliefs common to all Christians but also to particular emphases or historic distinctives distinguishing that group from others. The only problem latent in this practice is that those signing the statement might begin to look down on those who could not sign. For example, some seminaries have asked their faculty members, or even their graduating students, to sign an elaborate doctrinal statement that includes the teaching that Christ is going to return to the earth before the thousand-year millennial kingdom. This, in my view, is a clear example of a persuasion-level belief. An individual does not have to believe this in order to be a true Christian. However, I have no problem with this or any other nonconviction-level teaching being included in an institution's boundary statement as long as it is clear that one can be a genuine Christian without believing this particular nonessential teaching.

Avoiding Confusing Conclusions

The young man was shrinking down into his seat as he listened to the persuasive voice of the speaker. *I haven't even finished college,* the young man thought. *I want to get married, have children, travel. I'm not ready for the end of the world!*

The speaker continued to detail recent world events: tensions in the Middle East had again erupted into armed conflict between Israel and its neighbors; Russia was threatening to intervene; famine and earthquakes were on the increase around the globe. Then the climax of the message: the speaker paused dramatically and almost whispered, "I'll be surprised if this summer comes and Christ has not yet returned for His saints in the air."

It must be true. He seems so confident; he knows so much about the Bible. The young man believed the speaker when he said Jesus would come back before summer. Why? Because of the authoritative way the speaker asserted all his beliefs as if they were convictions.

I know this was the young man's reaction because that young man was me! The year was 1967. And, of course, Jesus did not return by the summer of '67, in the air or any other way. Fortunately, my baby faith wasn't severely damaged by this dogmatic, prophetic teaching. However, a confusion of conviction- and persuasion-level beliefs can have serious consequences.

I have known nonbelievers who listened to messages like the one I heard and said, "He's returning by summer? We'll just wait and see!" Then later they scoffed, "I knew the Bible wasn't true." I believe we all, as Christians, have a responsibility to distinguish between those central points about which the Bible is clear (and about which nearly all Christians agree) and those concepts that are peripheral or questionable.

Not only does a failure to distinguish between crucial and less crucial beliefs sometimes keep people from coming to Christ, but that failure can hurt even our own walks as Christians. I often shudder when I hear Christian brothers or sisters speak of their own pet theories as if they had a certain word from the Lord. The reason it frightens me is that I have known several believers who seemed to hold everything they believed at the same high level of dogmatic conviction. When they told you which Bible translation you should read, it was with the same intensity and tone of voice they used when they talked about the deity of Christ. When I met these same people several years later, they had ceased believing in Christ or the Bible at all.

As I talked with them, trying to understand how they had lost their faith, it seemed to me they had set themselves up for a fall. They were expending so much mental and emotional energy trying to hold vast numbers of questionable ideas at the highest level of conviction that it took very little to rattle their system and bring the whole thing crashing down. In their minds, either it was all true or none of it was true. When someone, perhaps even a well-meaning Christian, convinced them that one of their "convictions" was wrong, the whole shaky edifice became suspect and eventually they could trust none of it. Oddly enough, one of the best ways to protect your faith may be to learn to take some of what you believe less seriously.

If we are going to love God with our minds as well as our hearts, if we are going to worship Him "in spirit and truth,"[27] then we must have some way to sort out what is crucial to our Christian faith from what is helpful but secondary, or even optional or questionable. I have personally found that the convictions-persuasions-opinions paradigm gives me confidence that I am listening intently to those things God Himself deems most important without becoming overly distracted by peripheral issues.

In the next two chapters, we will embark on a journey toward knowing God better by looking at what God has told us about Himself. We will begin by answering the question "Can we know that God exists?"

■ FOR PERSONAL REFLECTION ■

1. What is your immediate reaction when you hear the word "doctrine" or the word "theology"?
2. What is the connection between knowing about someone and knowing him or her in a personal way?
3. Before reading this chapter, what Christian beliefs did you hold at a conviction level? Make a list and put it somewhere for reference later as you continue through this book.

4. Have you ever observed Christians fighting or breaking fellowship over issues that should have been treated as persuasions or opinions? How should they have handled their disagreements?
5. Does your church (or denomination or Christian organization) have a "boundary statement"? Obtain a copy of it and see if you can classify the various points into the three levels of belief.

■ GROUP DISCUSSION GUIDE ■

1. Brainstorm: What are some beliefs that we should treat as convictions? (Don't evaluate; just have someone write down a list of possible convictions.)
2. What are some of the differences between convictions and persuasions as described in the first chapter?
3. What are some of the differences between persuasions and opinions?
4. What are some problems that might be solved if more Christians distinguished among these three levels of belief?
5. What are some ways it might help each of us personally if we made this distinction?
6. What are some doctrinal beliefs that we're not exactly sure how to classify? (Refer to the list from question 1. Make a new list of beliefs that the group is unsure how to classify or disagrees about. Save this new list for future discussion.)

■ RECOMMENDED READING ■

Note: the reading suggestions in this book fall into three main levels: beginning (for popular, adult-level reading); intermediate (for serious inquiry at the college or Bible school level); advanced (scholarly reading for graduate-level theology students).

Bruce Bickel and Stan Jantz, *Bruce & Stan's Guide to God* (Eugene, Oreg.: Harvest House, 1997). Appropriate for junior-high or high-school students, this book is soundly evangelical and easily readable and it covers all the areas of doctrine, including a chapter on the Christian life. The book employs the first person and uses many icons, text boxes, and other graphic devices to stimulate interest. Beginning.

Gilbert Bilezikian, *Christianity 101* (Grand Rapids, Mich.: Zondervan, 1993). Written by a Wheaton College professor, this book omits the crucial subjects of angels, Satan, demons, and the Christian walk but has brief, helpful chapters on the other areas of doctrine. Intermediate.

Paul Enns, *The Moody Handbook of Theology* (Chicago: Moody, 1989). This is an excellent overall resource covering all the areas of doctrine in 250 pages. In addition, Enns includes excellent sections on biblical, historical, dogmatic (traditional), and contemporary theology. Intermediate.

Millard J. Erickson, *Christian Theology* (Grand Rapids, Mich.: Baker, 1983–1985). If I could recommend only one complete systematic theology, I would recommend Erickson. His treatment is thorough, philosophically sophisticated, quite readable, and often devotional. Intermediate-advanced.

Wayne Grudem, *Systematic Theology* (Grand Rapids, Mich.: Zondervan, 1994). The most readable of today's evangelical academic theologians, Grudem defends a Reformed soteriology but is open to the miraculous gifts of the Spirit. Intermediate-advanced.

J. P. Moreland, *Love Your God with All Your Mind* (Colorado Springs, Colo.: NavPress, 1997). Evangelical philosopher Moreland makes an eloquent case for the role of the mind in the lives of believers. Intermediate.

Charles C. Ryrie, *Basic Theology* (Wheaton, Ill.: Victor, 1987). In this concise systematic theology, dispensational theologian Ryrie gives a biblically sound coverage of all the doctrinal areas. Intermediate.

Charles C. Ryrie, *A Survey of Bible Doctrine* (Chicago: Moody, 1972). This concise (191 pages) but somewhat dry introduction covers all the areas of theology (except the Christian walk) and cites many biblical references. Intermediate.

Bruce L. Shelley, *Theology for Ordinary People* (Downers Grove, Ill.: InterVarsity, 1993). Church-history professor Shelley has written a highly accessible two-hundred-page summary of all of the doctrines (including a chapter on the Christian life). Beginning-intermediate.

CHAPTER TWO

OUR GOD:
THE ONE WHO EXISTS

IT FELT LIKE SOME BIZARRE DREAM, BUT IT WAS REAL AND I WAS fully awake. I was sitting on the front seat of a bus headed for downtown Moscow in May of 1991, one of the final months of the Soviet empire. Seated next to me was an imposing official of the Russian Ministry of Education.

"You know," said the official, his face impassive, "in order to receive my doctorate, I had to pass a high-level exam on 'The Principles of Scientific Atheism.'" The official knew I was a Christian. In fact, his superior, the Russian Minister of Education, had invited me, as a member of an international team of Christian scholars, to introduce Russian public school teachers to a course we had written on Christian ethics and morality.

"It must be hard for you to work with all us atheists!" he said.

I wondered how to respond. I knew this man was to accompany us to the three cities where we were scheduled to hold teacher-training conferences. I had been warned that he had the power to pull the plug on the entire project at any point.

So . . . is he just testing me?

CAN WE PROVE GOD EXISTS?

Atheistic societies are actually a modern invention. It is only very recently in the history of the world that governments have tried to base entire nations and their systems of law on the assumption that there is no God. So it is no surprise that most of the individual Russian citizens I met believed in astrology, spiritualism, and UFOs. Even when taught the opposite, the human heart intuitively knows there is some higher power ordering and influencing our earthly lives. I discovered in 1991 that three-quarters of a century of communism had created in the hearts of the Russian people an intense hunger to answer the question "Is God real?"

The Bible tells us that God Himself left evidence in the world of His own existence. Paul said of the Gentile nations, "That which is known about God is evident within them; for God made it evident to them."[1] There is a kind of internal witness inside of each person that God exists. God also offers ample evidence of His existence, and even something of His nature, in the world around us. King David wrote, "The heavens are telling of the glory of God; and their expanse is declaring the work of His hands."[2] Because of these kinds of evidence, available to all people, nearly all societies in all times have believed in some higher supernatural being or beings. Most countries (and tribes) have had official deities or religions. So the first response a Christian can give to the skeptic is to ask, "How likely is it that the vast majority of people, in every culture today and throughout history, are wrong?" We Christians can sometimes feel as though we're in the minority, but when it comes to belief in God or a higher power, our view is the overwhelming majority opinion.[3]

However, some people are indeed atheists like my Russian friend, the Soviet official. How can that be, if the evidence that God exists is all around us and even inside of us? Paul explained the process by which individuals or even whole cultures come to the point of sincerely denying what is obviously true. "Even though they knew God, they did not honor Him as God, or give thanks; but they became futile in their speculations, and their foolish heart was darkened."[4] The result is what we might call "brilliant foolishness." David declared, "The fool has said in his heart, 'There is no God.'"[5] Paul concurred that, "professing to be wise, they became fools."[6] Clearly this is a conviction-level issue. If God does not exist, then Christ could not be God, and He cannot be our hope of salvation.

Nevertheless, I have met many Christians in the United States who feel embarrassed or ashamed of their faith. It's not that they themselves doubt God's existence. Rather, they fear that the idea of God will seem foolish or intellectually naïve to their educated friends. But embarrassment need not rule! I often have seen good answers to the question of God's existence give Christians the confidence they need to talk to those who don't yet know Christ.

Through the centuries Christians have suggested a number of arguments to show that a God like the one portrayed in the Bible does exist. Some of these arguments appear in seed form in the Bible itself. Others are the invention of Christian philosophers of the past. While these arguments may not prove God's existence beyond question, and while they will not convince everyone, they can be helpful when we respond to atheists, agnostics, and believers in other religions who worship a god quite different from the God of the Bible. Additionally, these arguments can strengthen our faith and the faith of new Christians.

The Cosmological Argument: Cause and Effect

Our normal experience of the world tells us that everything has some kind of cause. If I see a pencil mark on a piece of paper, I know something or someone caused it. Maybe someone marked on the paper to test a pencil. Maybe a pencil accidentally fell and marked the paper. But it would be ridiculous to say, "The pencil mark is just there; no pencil caused it."

The argument from cause and effect begins by stating that every effect must have a cause. Each of those causes must itself have a prior cause. If we follow this line of logic back far enough, we reach a point where we have two choices. We can say there is an unending chain of causes that goes back forever and has no beginning (philosophers call this "infinite regress"). Or we can say there must have been a "first cause" that was not itself caused by something prior. Christians (and other theists such as Jews and Muslims) believe it is more reasonable to say there was a first cause (God) who started the whole chain of cause and effect.

Skeptics are fond of asking, "But who caused God?" The answer is "No one." If God Himself had a cause, then He would not be the "first cause" but at least the second. The question remains: Is there really any way to say which is more likely, that there was a first cause, or an endless chain of cause and effect going back forever?

I believe there is considerable scientific evidence to indicate that the "first cause" view is the more likely explanation. Nearly all scientists in the world today support what is known as the big bang theory of the universe.[7] According to this widely held view, everything we now see in the universe began as an immense explosion of energy about twelve to thirteen billion years ago.[8] But scientists are unable to come up with any natural explanation of what or who caused the big bang itself. According to Einstein's general theory of relativity, time itself began at the moment of the big bang. This would seem to be a powerful argument against the idea of infinite regress and a compelling argument for a first cause. Robert Jastrow, the astronomer who founded NASA's Goddard Institute for Space Studies, puts it this way:

> For the scientist who has lived by his faith in the power
> of reason, the story ends like a bad dream. He has scaled
> the mountains of ignorance; he is about to conquer the

highest peak; as he pulls himself over the final rock, he is greeted by a band of theologians who have been sitting there for centuries.[9]

Even from the viewpoint of impartial science, it is now far more reasonable to say the universe had a first cause than to try to argue for an unending chain of cause and effect reaching back forever. However, the cosmological argument doesn't tell us anything about what God is like, only that there must be an "uncaused cause."

The Teleological Argument: Order and Design

Christians also can point out that the particular type of universe we live in is evidence for the existence of God. This is called the argument from design or the "teleological argument."[10] The cosmological argument begins with the simple observation that *something* exists rather than *nothing*. In contrast, the teleological argument observes that the things we see in the universe are highly complex and serve specific purposes.

While this argument was stated in seed form by Plato, it was popularized by William Paley (1743–1805) in his famous watchmaker analogy. Paley asked us to imagine crossing a field and stubbing our foot against a stone. If we were to wonder how the stone came to be there, he said, it would not be hard to imagine that it had always lain there in that field. But if we found a watch lying in the field, it would be difficult to believe it was "just there." The watch is intricate, and every part is necessary for a specific purpose—telling time. It would be absurd to deny that the watch had an intelligent designer, a watchmaker. In the same way, Paley argued, the world shows evidence of purpose and, therefore, of intelligent design. The only adequate explanation for the type of world we see is that behind it is an intelligent Designer. Many see the Bible itself as using an argument from design in Psalm 19:1-4 and Acts 14:15-18.

A variation of the argument from design looks at the human

race.[11] Does it make sense, the argument goes, to believe that thinking, feeling, imaginative, aesthetic creatures such as humans come from a mechanism such as blind chance? Can impersonal forces give rise to personal beings? A Designer who is personal (thinking, feeling, moral, and so on) is the only adequate explanation for the existence of humanity. The advantage of this argument over the previous one is that it begins to show what kind of God must be behind creation. We are no longer talking about an abstract "first cause" but are now discussing a being who more closely resembles the God of the Bible.

The Ontological Argument: From Idea to Reality
One of the most subtle and difficult (but also one of the most fascinating) arguments for God's existence is the "ontological argument."[12] This argument was first proposed by Anselm, archbishop of Canterbury (1033–1109). Here is my summary of the argument:

1. The idea of a perfect being exists.
2. To be "perfect," God must be greater than any other being we could conceive.
3. A real God would be greater than an imaginary one.
4. God cannot exist only in imagination, for then He would not be the perfect being.
5. Therefore, God must exist in reality.

What this argument basically says is that to believe God exists only in our imagination is a logical contradiction (because I can conceive of a greater being than the imaginary God, that is, a real one). It is irrational and self-contradictory to believe that God is merely the product of human imagination.

It has been my privilege to teach theology classes to thousands of graduate students for more than twenty years. During that time, I have noticed that nearly all of those students felt there was something wrong with the ontological argument. This is not because they disbelieve God's existence. Most of my students are committed Christians, many of them full-time Christian workers. As one bright young woman put it, "I feel as though Anselm is playing a shell game with me—I carefully watch all his moves, but the pea ends up under the wrong shell."

I think part of the problem for us in contemporary society is that we've been conditioned to think inductively rather than deductively. We are used to the scientific method in which we first consider a series of specific facts (data) and then work our way up to a generalization. Both the argument from cause and effect and the argument from design are inductive. They begin by observing something about the universe, and then they work their way up to a generalization: God exists.

The argument from being, however, goes in the opposite direction. It begins by asking us to assume some general principles. Specifically, the ontological argument asks us to accept at the outset that a real being is greater than an imaginary one. Then, through logical deduction, Anselm worked his way down to a specific: God must really exist. This kind of deductive logic was commonly accepted by philosophers and theologians in the Middle Ages but is less familiar, and therefore less convincing, today.

In fact, many criticisms of the ontological argument have arisen during the past several centuries. The nineteenth-century philosopher Immanuel Kant accused Anselm of making a categorical error. Kant believed that "existence" is not a property that can be added to a thing to perfect it. But my opinion is that you will find this argument convincing if you can accept the idea that a real God is greater than an imaginary one. If you accept that idea, then the rest of the argument is logical. If you reject it, then with Kant you will likely conclude that the argument is flawed.[13]

The Argument from Religious Experience

Some people today (both ordinary folks and professional philosophers) find the previous three types of argument unconvincing or irrelevant. However, many people in the Western world find another argument quite convincing—the argument from experience. In its simplest form, the argument goes like this:

1. People from every nation and culture of the world claim to have experienced God or some higher reality.
2. They can't all be misled or deluded.
3. Therefore, some kind of God or higher power must exist.

Critics of this argument have at least two objections, both of which center on the fact that religious experiences from various cultures yield wildly varying descriptions of God.

Objection 1: Experiences of God are contradictory. I first became aware of this difficulty as a young Campus Crusade staff member when I tried to share my faith with a Mormon missionary. After a frustrating hour, I finally asked, "How do you know that Mormonism is true?"

I'll never forget his answer. "I prayed and asked God to show me if the Book of Mormon was true or not; then I experienced a 'burning in my bosom,' and I knew that it was true!" How could I answer him? I couldn't deny that he had the experience. How could I argue that my experience of Christ changing my life was more valid than his experience of a burning bosom? Yet his experience led him to believe there are many gods and that he can become one himself someday. Mine led me to believe I am a finite creation of a unique Creator. Based on the fact that we both had religious experiences, how could we determine whose belief was right?

Objection 2: Beliefs color experience. This objection argues that religious belief does not arise directly from religious experience. Rather, we interpret our religious experience within our particular cultural and religious context. We bring our cultural conditioning, including our idea of God, to all our experience, including religious experience.[14]

How do we respond to these two objections? As Christians, we believe that we have experienced God's forgiveness in Christ, have received answers to prayer, and have heard His "still, small voice." Do these objections mean our experience is invalid? In general, I think we must acknowledge that there is some truth in both objections. The fact that I have had a religious experience does not prove everything I believe, and no experience happens in a cultural or religious vacuum.

But now let me deal more specifically with the second objection first. While it is true that my previous belief system will color my experience, it does not necessarily follow that nothing new can ever be learned from religious experience. Paul changed from an enemy to an advocate of Christ as a result of one brief encounter (see Acts 9). Peter was cleansed of lifelong racial prejudice by a single vision (see Acts 10). My own religious experience in college played a decisive role in my change from a vague pantheist to an ardent Christian. My own cultural and intellectual grid should have led me to have a pantheistic experience of "unity with the god who is everything." Instead, I experienced a distinct, personal being of awesome beauty and power. While it is undoubtedly true that our culture and religious training affect our interpretation, this doesn't mean that God is unable to break through cultural conditioning and influence what we think and feel as a result of religious experience.

Then there is the objection that people who claim religious experiences sometimes hold contradictory beliefs. Here I think it's important to distinguish between what the argument from religious experience tends to prove and what it does not. In my view, the fact of transcultural religious experience is a crippling blow to atheism. The universality of religious experience lends powerful credibility to the idea that there is *some kind* of higher being or power. However, I do not believe we can logically determine (from this argument alone) the nature of that power or being. The argument from religious experience can, in my view, be a powerful apologetic for biblical Christianity when used in conjunction with other arguments (such as the personal version of the design argument given above).

What about the Mormon missionary? What would I say if I ran into him today? I think I would say something like this: "Your experience of a burning in your bosom does not, by itself, prove the truth of Mormonism any more than my experience, taken alone, proves the doctrine that salvation is by grace through faith. So let's look for some other, more objective kind of evidence that might indicate which of our beliefs is more likely to be true." I would then take him to the historical evidence that Jesus' words are true and that the Bible is the Word of God (see chapters 5 and 6).[15]

I want to make one final observation before we leave the subject of personal experience. In the past thirty years of ministry, I have found that one of the most compelling forms of evangelism is an individual, personal testimony. In one sense, a testimony is an argument from personal experience. The implicit argument is something like this: "If Christ has changed my life, then God must exist and Christianity must be true." I have just said it is not logical to reach such a conclusion from the simple fact of religious experience. Why, then, is a personal testimony so convincing to so many nonbelievers? I think there are at least two reasons.

First, during my lifetime there has been an erosion of confidence in logic and the scientific method as a means of discovering truth. While older adults from the so-called "builder" generation (those born before World War II) retain a high confidence in technology, the "baby boomers" (born between the war and the early sixties) tend to be more skeptical of "progress" and the power of science to solve our problems. As a group, the newest generation of adults (those born since the early sixties)[16] have grown even less confident in logic and the results of scientific progress. Highly publicized, controversial court decisions have fed a growing cynicism that "you can prove anything with a good argument."[17] Increasingly, educated people, especially the younger generation, are drawn to emotion, story, mysticism, and personal experience as means of finding truth.[18]

A second reason for the power of a personal testimony is that hearing an individual's story is an opportunity to identify with a whole person: body, emotion, conscience, and will, as well as mind. While a person's story may imply a logical argument, the appeal is to my person as a whole, not merely to my mind.

How was I myself persuaded to become a Christian? As a skeptical college student, I was drawn to Christ not primarily by logical argument but by the testimony and life example of believers. I met some "born-again Christians" through my college choir during my freshman year, but they didn't impress me. They struck me as intellectual lightweights, and it did not surprise me they would believe something as foolish as Christianity. Then in my sophomore year, I was invited to a meeting of college students in a private home. The speaker was Bud Hinkson.[19] Bud was articulate, educated, and funny.

As an aspiring performer (I was then a music major), I was impressed with the way Bud captured and held an audience. However, to this day I cannot remember a single thing he said about Christ or the Bible. After his talk, Bud made a beeline for me (I think someone had told him I wasn't a believer), and we talked for more than an hour. With him was a young man named Ken, a disciple who was accompanying Bud in his travels. Bud took out a pen and began drawing some diagrams on a paper napkin. I have no memory of what he said or wrote on the napkin, except that several times during the conversation I took the pen away from him and changed the diagram he was drawing to the way I thought it should be.[20]

Though I was not at all convinced by what he was saying, I was impressed by Bud. Several times during the conversation, Bud turned and said something to Ken with a big grin on his face. Once or twice he put his arm around Ken and gave him a spontaneous, manly hug. I was drawn by the obvious healthy love between these two men. The next morning at breakfast I said to my mom, "These Christians—the things they believe are crazy, but . . . there's just something about them." I was drawn to Christ, not primarily by some logical argument, but through personal testimony and the captivating Christian character of Bud and other genuine believers.

DOES GOD'S EXISTENCE MATTER?

The belief that God exists is a conviction-level belief. However, belief in the truth or usefulness of the various arguments is a matter of persuasion or opinion. What, then, is the value of arguments for the existence of God? At the end of the last century some philosophers declared that these traditional proofs had been refuted and were dead. But the twentieth century, particularly the last fifty years or so, has seen an incredible revival of interest in the arguments on the part of professional philosophers.[21] Some nonbelievers find that one or more of these arguments makes Christianity credible enough to warrant further investigation.[22] Additionally, the doubts of many new believers have been assuaged or removed by these forms of thinking.

What about the atheistic Russian official? I'd like to say he was wonderfully converted, perhaps by one of the traditional proofs for God's existence. However, life is more complex and open-ended than we might like. Almost a month later I walked with him to his train in Leningrad (soon renamed St. Petersburg), which would take him back to his home in Moscow. During our days together, he had warmed to me and the other Christians and had given us his blessing to take our teacher training all over Russia. He gave me the traditional Russian bear hug and stepped on the train still an atheist. Despite my attempts to contact him on subsequent trips, we have lost touch. I often wonder if the seeds I and others planted on that first Russian trip have borne fruit in his life. However, during that month, hundreds of other teachers and educational administrators indicated that they received

Christ as their Lord.[23] In this country, which had virtually worshiped science for seventy-five years, many of the teachers told us they were astonished and deeply impressed to hear us present logical arguments for the reality of the Christian God.

Having confidence that there are good reasons to believe in God's existence can comfort us in our own times of doubt or discouragement and can give us boldness to share our experience with nonbelievers. Even though I initially came to Christ because I was impressed by the character and testimonies of Christians, as soon as I received Christ, I began to have intellectual doubts.

My first siege of doubt struck just a few weeks after I received Christ. I'm grateful my friend Bud Hinkson was again there to give me the encouragement I needed. I was attending a training conference for new believers held during the Christmas break. On the third night it was announced that the next morning we would all pile into buses, drive to the southern California beaches, and spend the day sharing our faith. This threw me into a panic. *Do I really believe all this enough to spend the day sharing it with strangers?* Suddenly, all I could think about were my own doubts and questions. I went to the front desk of the hotel and paged Bud. He graciously left an important meeting and spent the next hour talking with me in the hotel lobby.

"How can we be sure all this God stuff isn't just our imagination?" I asked. "Maybe we've all been talked into seeing the world in a religious way. How do we know all these 'answers to prayer' aren't just coincidence?"

Bud leaned back in his chair, smiled at me, and shook his head.

"Alan, when you've seen as much as I have, you won't wonder that anymore." He went on to tell me example after example of answers to prayer and of times he had seen God supernaturally intervene in his life. He concluded, "After all the Lord has taken me through, I can't possibly have doubts about whether He's real."

As a young Christian, I found Bud's response to be just what I needed. Bud didn't call his answer "the argument from religious experience," but essentially that's what it was. I was able to lean on his experience of God and get on the bus the next morning. Arguments like the ones presented in this chapter often have been a great encouragement to my feeble faith. Early in my Christian life they helped me begin confidently enjoying God and His Word.

In the next chapter we'll explore more about the God we are coming to know and enjoy. We will try to answer the question "Who is this God who actually exists?"

■ FOR PERSONAL REFLECTION ■

1. Have you ever seriously questioned whether God exists? What caused your doubts? What has helped you overcome them?
2. In your opinion, is it possible for doubts to lead to spiritual growth? Why or why not?
3. Do you know anyone who is a true atheist (does not believe in any sort of God or higher power)? What type of lifestyle would be most consistent for a person with such a philosophy?
4. Which kinds of evidence discussed in this chapter would be most convincing to the nonbelievers you know? Why?
5. Which kinds of evidence would be the most comfort and/or encouragement to you, personally, in times of doubt?

■ GROUP DISCUSSION GUIDE ■

1. Hot seat: You, or someone you select, "play" a skeptic who is not sure God exists. Have a volunteer try to answer the skeptic's objections. When the role play is done, have other

members of the group give their suggestions of other things the volunteer might have said.

2. Which of the arguments for God's existence do you find most convincing and why?

3. Has there ever been a time when any of you doubted that God existed? (If none has, ask: Does anyone know family members, friends, or coworkers who doubt that God exists?) What has (or would) help you (or your friend) overcome doubts about God?

4. Are there some specific people we can begin to pray for, that they will be able to overcome their doubts about God?

■ RECOMMENDED READING ■

M. A. Corey, *God and the New Cosmology: The Anthropic Design Argument* (Lanham, Md.: Rowman & Littlefield, 1993). This is a thorough, convincing update of the teleological argument. While Corey includes many biblical allusions, he argues only for a theistic creator, not an explicitly Christian God. Intermediate.

Kevin Graham Ford, *Jesus for a New Generation: Putting the Gospel in the Language of Xers* (Downers Grove, Ill.: InterVarsity, 1995). Ford, the son of evangelist Leighton Ford, has done the best job to date of analyzing the generation born since the early 1960s and giving practical suggestions for bringing them to Christ. The book is written in the narrative style Ford recommends for approaching the current generation. Beginning-intermediate.

C. S. Lewis, *Mere Christianity* (New York: Macmillan, 1952). Lewis's classic is one of the most widely read and quoted apologetics of the twentieth century. He relies mainly on a version of the argument from personal experience (the moral argument) but artfully weaves in various of the other theistic proofs. Intermediate.

J. P. Moreland, ed., *The Creation Hypothesis: Scientific Evidence for an Intelligent Designer* (Downers Grove, Ill.: InterVarsity, 1994). A collection of articles focusing on arguments for design from various scientific disciplines. Includes chapters by philosopher of science Stephen Meyer, biochemist John Omdahl, astronomer Hugh Ross, and paleontologist Kurt P. Wise. Advanced.

J. P. Moreland and Kai Nielsen, *Does God Exist: The Great Debate* (Nashville, Tenn.: Nelson, 1990). Based on an actual debate in 1988 at the University of Mississippi, the volume also includes new articles by atheist Nielsen and Christian philosopher Moreland, as well as some by other noted theists and atheists. Intermediate.

Alvin C. Plantinga, *God, Freedom and Evil* (Grand Rapids, Mich.: Eerdmans, 1974). In the second half of this book, prominent philosopher of religion Plantinga gives a rigorous contemporary defense of the cosmological, teleological, and ontological arguments. Advanced.

Louis P. Pojman, ed., *Philosophy of Religion: An Anthology* (Belmont, Calif.: Wadsworth, 1987). Evangelical philosopher Pojman has assembled an excellent collection of essays and book selections, including arguments for and against all of the classic proofs of God's existence. The book also includes sections on faith versus reason, miracles, and immortality. Designed as an introductory college text, the volume contains some graduate-level articles. Intermediate-advanced.

CHAPTER THREE

OUR GOD: WHO HE IS

"WHY WOULDN'T YOU CONSIDER BECOMING A CHRISTIAN?" I was sitting with Sarah on the couch in her parents' front room. It was the first time we had seen each other in three years, and the memories of our turbulent, six-month-long high-school romance flooded back. At one time I was so taken with her dark beauty, her intelligence, and her sarcastic humor that I had attended temple with her and even talked to her rabbi about converting to Judaism. (He had strongly and wisely discouraged me.)

"A lot of reasons," she said with the same ironic half smile that had wrenched my heart so often in the past.

"Name one," I said.

"Well . . . you have three gods, and we Jews worship only one."

I had become a Christian only a few months before, but I knew there was something wrong with what she was saying.

"No . . . no," I stammered. "We only worship one God— the same God as you."

"Well . . ." she mused, and there was a twitch at the corner of her mouth. I had been on the debate team in high school, but I'd never won an argument with Sarah. And when the twitch kicked in, I knew I was in trouble. "You believe that Christ was God, don't you?"

"Yes, but . . . "

"And the Holy Ghost—it's God too, isn't it?"

"I guess so, but . . . "

"Father, Son, and Holy Ghost—you've got three gods!" Sarah leaned back in her corner of the couch and crossed her arms.

How Many Gods?

Our little discussion on that couch actually had a long history—a debate about the nature of the Christians' God stretching back to the very beginnings of the church. In the early centuries of Christianity, believers faced a series of difficult challenges to their teachings. They knew that Jesus' miracles, particularly His resurrection and His own teachings about Himself, set Him apart from any ordinary man. They also established the practice, early on, of baptizing "in the name of the Father, Son, and Holy Spirit."[1] However, the Christians in the first few centuries weren't very precise in their statements of the relations among these three divine persons.[2] As in the case of many Christian teachings, God used heretical challenges from within the church to stimulate a clear formulation of doctrine, in this case the doctrine of the Trinity.

One of the first challenges came from a teacher named Praxeus who held a view called "monarchianism." The largest division of these monarchians saw Jesus and the Holy Spirit as simply modes, or faces, of the one God. These heretical Christians were Jewish in their view of God except that they simply had three different names for the one God. This sent the Christian leaders back to the New Testament to read it more carefully.

"No," they declared, "there is more to the difference between

Father, Son, and Holy Spirit than the monarchians are saying." In answer to Praxeus, the church father Tertullian (about A.D. 165–220) coined the word "Trinity" to signify that each of the persons was individually God.[3]

A later challenge that further clarified the doctrine came from Arianism. Arius (about 250–336) saw the Father as eternal but said that the Son and Holy Spirit had a beginning. Athanasius (about 296–373) responded that the three persons were coeternal. Ultimately, two church councils (Nicaea in 325 and Constantinople in 381) formulated the language that the Bible-believing church has overwhelmingly accepted ever since: one God in three persons.

Three Persons
Through the centuries Christians have resorted to many analogies in trying to explain the doctrine of the Trinity. Some have said it is like ice, water, and steam—all are H_2O. Others have suggested the analogy of the sun, its light, and its power. Still others have said it's like a one-man show in a theater: God comes on the stage of the world first in a long beard and plays the part of a severe father; next he changes into the youthful makeup of a compassionate son; finally fog rolls across the stage and we hear His disembodied voice as a mysterious spirit.

The difficulty with such analogies is that they all break down. Most analogies for the Trinity, if carried too far, lead to modalism, similar to the views of the monarchians.[4] Modalism says there is one God who, at various times, wears three separate masks or plays three different roles. What is wrong with this view? The reason this view was rejected by the early church (and we should reject it as well) is that it is not true to the way God is presented in the New Testament.

So what is the biblical picture? At the baptism of Jesus, the Father spoke audibly to the Son, and the Holy Spirit visibly descended in the form of a dove.[5] This seems like genuine interaction, not simply one God playing three roles. Jesus spent long hours in prayer to the Father. Why did He do this? Some have suggested it was to be an example to us. However, if He was only play-acting—if He did not genuinely desire and need to do this—then the narrative loses much of its power. The early church concluded that what we see in the pages of the Gospels is a true relationship between two persons, the Father and His Son. The most poignant encounter between the two came in Gethsemane. Jesus prayed, "Not as I will, but as Thou wilt." These two persons were so separate that they could have different wills! Jesus' will was to avoid the cross, but He submitted to the Father's will, which was for the Son to die.

One God

What about my friend's charge that we Christians worship three gods? The difficulty with this view, and the reason similar ideas were rejected in the early centuries of Christianity, is that the New Testament is clear in its endorsement of the idea that there is one, and only one, God. In combating the paganism and idolatry of Corinth, Paul asserted that "there is no such thing as an idol in the world, and that there is no God but one."[6]

How shall we define the doctrine of the Trinity? Many biblical theologians have attempted clear and unambiguous definitions through the years, but I particularly like a recent formulation by Wayne Grudem. "God eternally exists as three persons, Father, Son, and Holy Spirit, and each person is fully God, and there is one God."[7] Believers through the centuries—Orthodox, Catholic, and Protestant—have agreed that the Trinity is a doctrine crucial to historical biblical Christianity. Therefore, I class it as a conviction-level belief.

Why is belief in the Trinity so important? For one thing, it is a crucial part of what makes Christianity unique. Several other religions declare that there is only one God.[8] But in most of these religions, God is distant, usually severe, and ultimately unknowable in an intimate and personal way. On the other hand, there are many religions, particularly Greek, Roman, and

Norse mythology, in which the gods are quite personal and do have intimate relations with humans.[9] But these gods are finite and betray many humanlike flaws such as foolishness, petty jealousy, lust, and pride.

Only in Christianity do we find a God who is both infinite and fully personal. Without the Trinity, God could not have come in the form of a man and yet still be the one true God. Without the Trinity, Jesus could not have died for our sins by being separated from the Father and yet still be God Himself at the same time. While the Trinity is, in many ways, a mysterious doctrine that no human mind can fully comprehend, it stands at the very center of the Christian faith. Without it, Christ's deity and our own salvation would be lost. When, therefore, someone asks the question "Who is God?" the Christian answers, "There is only one God who has eternally existed in three persons, the Father, the Son, and the Holy Spirit."

What Is God Like?

"Let me ask you something." The student took a sip of his Coke and set the paper cup down on the long, rectangular table of the student union lunchroom. "Can God create a rock so big He can't lift it?"

"Of course . . ." I said slowly. Then I thought a moment. I'd never heard the question before, but as a new staff member with Campus Crusade for Christ, I wanted desperately for this skeptical student to think I knew what I was talking about.

"Er . . . no. He could lift any size rock, so . . ."

The student laughed.

"See, that's what I mean. Christianity just doesn't make sense!"

He Tells Us About Himself

This young, blossoming skeptic actually raised important questions we all need to answer. Exactly who is the God we worship?

What can He do? Can He do anything? What is He really like?

When Christian theologians ask what God is like, they usually form the answer in a discussion of God's "attributes." An attribute is anything that someone says about (attributes to) another person. In the case of evangelical theology, we are interested in what the Bible attributes to (says is true of) God. In the next two chapters, we will see that God the Holy Spirit is the coauthor of all of Scripture. In one sense, then, we are asking, "What things has God said are true about (attributed to) Himself?"

Theologians normally classify God's attributes in two categories. The most common names for these divisions are "communicable" and "incommunicable" attributes.[10] Communicable attributes are those that God can transmit (or communicate) to created creatures. Therefore, love is a communicable attribute because humans (and angels) are capable of giving and receiving love. Eternality, on the other hand, is classified as an incommunicable attribute because all of God's creations began at a point in time and, therefore, only God is truly eternal.[11]

I prefer the classification suggested by Francis Schaeffer, who distinguished between God's infinite and personal attributes.[12]

He Is Infinite

Among God's infinite attributes are those things Scripture reserves for (or we can reasonably conclude belong to) God alone. Earlier we posed the question "Can God do anything?" I think the answer must be "No." If most theologians in history are right and there are certain attributes of God that are incommunicable, then we have discovered one thing God cannot do: He cannot transmit His infinite attributes to His finite creatures. God's infinite attributes include the "omnis" (omnipotence, omnipresence, omniscience, and so on), which were originally proposed by Greek philosophers before the time of the New Testament. I use them in my classes for convenience of communication, but their meanings must be defined strictly within the boundaries set by biblical revelation.[13]

The Bible indicates (and theologians have recognized) many different attributes of God. I am going to comment in some detail on four (two infinite and two personal) of the ones that have been the most controversial and that I think are most crucial to knowing and enjoying our relationship with God.

Omnipotence. To say that God is omnipotent means He has all power. God told Abram, "I am God Almighty."[14] The idea of having all might seems to correlate well with the idea of being "omnipotent."[15] The term "Almighty" is used of no one else in the Bible, implying it is an attribute belonging to God alone.[16] But is the idea of a being with all power inherently self-contradictory? Years after the student posed the question about God creating a rock He could not lift, I discovered that this question was not just a smart-aleck retort of skeptical undergraduates but that serious philosophers of religion have devoted dozens of scholarly journal articles to the question! Although there have been many answers proposed to the rock problem, the most reasonable seems to me to be the following. (I wish I had understood the problem well enough to give this response in that lunchroom!)

No, God can't create a rock so big that He cannot lift it. However, I do not think His inability to do this puts any limitation on His omnipotence. It's simply *logically impossible*. What the question poses is really nonsense, and a God who could (or would) perform nonsense tasks would not be a greater God but a lesser one.

Let me phrase the same answer in a different way. God can create a rock of any possible size. Name any size rock you wish and God can create it. God also can lift each of those rocks. The phrase "a rock so big God cannot lift it" sounds like it is naming something real or at least possible. However, when we analyze it in relation to God's attribute of being almighty, it is really an intrinsically impossible notion. What we are saying is "Can

God create something greater than Himself?" The answer is no, He cannot. He cannot even create something equal to Himself. Therefore, He has the power to control everything He creates (including each rock).

So, we have discovered something else that God cannot do. He cannot do anything that directly contradicts one of His attributes. God is the source of reason and order in our universe. The fact that He does not (and, in fact, cannot) perform non-sense tasks causes me to want to honor and worship Him more, but it is not a challenge to His power.

Immutability. God is unchanging and unchangeable. Through a prophet God declared, "I, the LORD, do not change."[17] James affirmed that with God "there is no varia-tion."[18] Unfortunately, beginning early in church history, many Christian theologians added to the biblical idea of changelessness the more negative notion of impassibility. ("Impassible" means that God is so unchangeable that He cannot be influenced by His creation, cannot even feel any-thing as a result of what we do.) These theologians didn't get this idea from the Bible but rather from Greek philosophy.

In fact the Bible presents a God who does interact with His creation, who does feel as a result of human action. The Holy Spirit is grieved by our sin.[19] Jesus felt sorrow over the fate of Jerusalem and wept at the death of a friend.[20] So perhaps we can best understand immutability by saying that God's character never changes but that His actions, and even His feelings, change in response to the actions of His creatures.[21]

I think it is crucial to enjoying our relationship with God that we see both that His character does not change and that His feelings do. If God's character could change, how could we trust Him? He might love us today and then, through no change in us, have a bad day and decide to punish us tomor-row. On the other hand, if God really could not be affected in any way by what we do, then the best we could hope for is a one-way relationship: God could influence us but we could never hope to have any effect on Him. But the combination of immutability in character and mutability (or passibility) in feeling makes it possible for Him to be the best friend and the most loving Father in all the universe. When I go alone into the quiet of my heart to pray, I know that the One who is listening will always be true to me and to Himself, will genuinely care about me, and can respond to what I feel and do and say.

Other infinite attributes. God's other incommunicable attributes include omniscience (He knows everything), eternality (He is beyond or outside of time), omnipresence (He is everywhere), and self-existence (He was not caused by something else). These, too, are ways in which God, the Trinity, is unique and alone in all the universe.

He Is Personal

God's personal attributes include aspects of His character that created beings can and do share in some measure. These communicable attributes form the basis of our fellowship and relationship with Him. Consider these:

Loving. The most central of God's personal attributes is love. John (who was called the beloved disciple) stated that "God is love" (1 John 4:8). Our salvation is a direct result of God's attribute of love (see John 3:16).

A particular objection to biblical Christianity centers on the relationship between this attribute of God and the infinite attribute of omnipotence that we considered above. This objection is often called "the problem of evil." Simply stated, the objection says:

1. A loving God would desire to eliminate evil and suffering.
2. An omnipotent God would be able to eliminate evil and suffering.
3. Evil and suffering have not been eliminated.
4. Therefore, either God is not loving or He is not omnipotent (or neither).

While evangelical (and other) theologians have proposed many possible solutions to this problem, one answer seems both true to Scripture and satisfying to most believers. This answer questions the opening statement above. Would a loving God necessarily desire to eliminate all evil and suffering? We spoke earlier about a number of things God cannot do. I would like to suggest another to add to the list. I believe God cannot create a world in which genuinely free moral agents (angels and humans) exist and in which there also will be no evil or suffering. In other words, God could create a world with no evil, but He would have to create that world without free moral agents. Or He could create a world with free moral agents but one that included evil. What He cannot do is create a world with free moral agents and no evil.[22]

I believe that God, acting in accordance with His attribute of love, chose to limit His omnipotence and create free moral agents. When human beings chose to turn away from Him and commit moral evil, God remained true to His choice and let them bring evil into the universe. I believe that in the end this will bring about a greater good than if God had chosen to create a perfectly good universe with no free moral agents.

Righteous. The word *righteous* comes from the word *right*. This simply means that God always does what is right. David declared, "The LORD is righteous in all His ways, and kind in all His deeds."[23] As a child of the sixties, I grew up assuming that God would be loving, but it was something of a shock to me as a new Christian to discover that God was also righteous. I think my problem was that I associated the word *righteous* with the idea of self-righteousness. I intensely disliked self-righteous people and, therefore, had trouble warming up to the idea that God was righteous.

As I began to read the New Testament, I discovered that "righteous" and "self-righteous" are not near companions but rather polar opposites. Jesus was genuinely righteous (always did what was right), but He was not an arrogant, self-centered braggart. Rather, He was humble and considerate and always sought to give the glory to His Father. In stark contrast to the truly righteous Jesus were the self-righteous Pharisees. I have had the privilege, a few times in my life, of spending time with someone who demonstrated a significant measure of Jesus' righteousness. I found these mature disciples a joy to be around. They were kind, considerate, warm, and genuinely interested in me. They gave me just a taste of why someone might "hunger and thirst after righteousness."[24]

Other personal attributes. Other aspects of the personal dimension of God's being include wisdom (He always exercises good judgment), goodness (He is free from all evil), holiness (He is unique and separated from all sin or impurity), freedom (He is not restrained by anything or anyone outside Himself), and mercy (He kindly chooses to be more than fair). These are attributes that God also has given some of His creatures. They are ways God desires us to be like Him and ways in which (when we are perfected) we will be like Him.

A number of God's infinite and personal attributes seem closely related to the doctrine of salvation and therefore candidates to be held at the conviction level. God's attributes of power, righteousness, and love seem particularly central to His desire and ability to save.

A TRUE IMAGE?

I mentioned that the decade in which I came of age (the sixties) made it harder for me to appreciate God's attribute of righteousness. Every one of us comes into our relationship with God having a less than perfect image of who He is. To further complicate matters, there is good evidence that we really have two kinds of images of God. First, we have a mental image of God that comes from what we have been taught and from what our logical reasoning about God tells us.

But we also have an emotional and perhaps even unconscious image, or picture, of what God is like.[25] This image is formed involuntarily out of our lifetime of experiences, particularly with those in authority over us, including our parents, older siblings, and other caretakers. Because none of these people are perfectly loving or righteous, because all of them fell short of treating us as Christ would have in their place, we develop a distorted emotional picture of God. Unfortunately, when we go alone to pray, the picture we have of the God who is listening is probably influenced more by our emotional image of God than by our conscious theology. If someone was abused by her earthly father, for example, she may have an irrational fear of God no matter how much she believes in her head that He is patient and loving.

How do we transform our image of God and bring it closer to who He really is? My mental image of God can be changed by a study of theology—by absorbing the material contained in this book, for example. However, my emotional image is not so easily changed, particularly if it was seriously distorted by a devastating emotional event such as sexual abuse by a parent. How can our emotional image be changed? The simple answer is that because our distorted view was formed by our emotional relationships with people, it must be re-formed by significant emotional relationships. Part of the reason Bud Hinkson and other godly men since have had such a powerful influence on my relationship with God is that my early relationship with my own earthly father was distant.[26] Although my childhood was a safe and happy one, I needed the reparenting of godly men who genuinely reflected aspects of God's character that I had not previously experienced.

What about people whose emotional image of God is more seriously distorted than mine was? For many believers a long-term, emotionally transparent relationship with one or more Christians who can mirror a more accurate picture of God is the key to gradually transforming a seriously distorted emotional image. One of the reasons Jesus encouraged us to pray with other believers, rather than always alone,[27] is that when we hear the heartfelt prayer of another believer, we also are catching an emotional glimpse of the character and attributes of the God to whom they are speaking.

One-on-one discipleship over many months (or years) can be an effective setting for this kind of reparenting. However, most Christians are more likely to find this kind of personal spiritual intimacy in a committed small group.[28] When someone's emotional God-image is severely damaged, help from a professional Christian counselor, perhaps in conjunction with a support group of those from a similar background, is often the only practical way to restore a healthy emotional image of God.[29]

In this chapter we have looked at some remarkable aspects of what God is like. We have pondered the teaching that God is three persons but still one God. We have learned that in God's infinite attributes, He is unique and quite unlike us and all His other creations. In His personal attributes, God is a model for his personal creations.[30] He is infinite and beyond us, even beyond our comprehension, but He is also personal and is gradually making us to be like Him. We've found we often need the help of other believers to develop an undistorted emotional image of God. As we begin to truly see what and who He is, we can respect Him, worship Him more deeply, and take greater joy in the way He has made us in His image.

How can we be confident that our view of God is the correct one? Nearly all of what we know about the Trinity and God's attributes comes from the Bible. But when we read the Bible, can we trust that it is actually God speaking to us? We will try to answer these questions in the next two chapters.

■ FOR PERSONAL REFLECTION ■

1. Do you think the early Christians were right in rejecting modalism (the idea that there is one God who just appears in three forms)? Why or why not?

2. What is your way of explaining how we Christians don't worship three gods? Do you have a favorite analogy for picturing the Trinity?
3. What practical difference would it make in your life if God were not all-powerful?
4. How would it change your relationship with God if He were not immutable (unchangeable)?
5. Do you think the world (and your own life) would be better if God were to stop all evil by eliminating human free will?
6. How do you feel about God being righteous? Does this make you want to draw closer to Him, or does it tend to push you away from Him?
7. In what ways has your own emotional image of God been shaped by your family experiences?

■ GROUP DISCUSSION GUIDE ■

1. Pair share: In pairs, have each person share at least one memory from childhood about God. (Did you think of God as a big man with a beard? Did you pray any prayers that were answered or not answered? How did you *feel* about God when you were little?)
2. What do you think of the idea that there are certain things God cannot do? Is anyone uncomfortable with saying that? Why or why not?
3. Can any of you think of ways that your emotional picture of God differs from what you believe to be true about Him? Explain.
4. Can you think of any people who have helped you form a more accurate emotional picture of God? What did they do, or what were they like, that helped you form a truer image of God?
5. What are some ways we in this group could help each other develop a better emotional image of God?

■ RECOMMENDED READING ■

James Montgomery Boice, *The Sovereign God* (Downers Grove, Ill.: InterVarsity, 1978). In chapters 9 through 14, this Presbyterian pastor sketches a sound and practical vision of the triune God and His attributes. The book also includes helpful chapters on the Bible and Creation. Intermediate.

Stephen T. Davis, ed., *Encountering Evil: Live Options in Theodicy* (Atlanta, Ga.: Knox, 1981). Edited by an evangelical philosopher who also wrote one of the chapters, this book presents and critiques five answers to the problem of evil from various perspectives, including process theology. Intermediate.

C. S. Lewis, *The Problem of Pain* (New York: Macmillan, 1962). Lewis makes a compelling and readable case that human pain (and even hell) are the only possible reality if there is to be true human freedom. Intermediate.

J. I. Packer, *Knowing God* (London: Hodder and Stoughton, 1973). Packer includes excellent chapters on various attributes of God. Intermediate.

Alvin Plantinga, *God, Freedom, and Evil* (New York: Harper & Row, 1974). Plantinga gives rigorous philosophical arguments for the "free-will defense." Advanced.

Francis A. Schaeffer, *The God Who Is There* (Chicago: InterVarsity, 1968). In this provocative and influential book, Schaeffer argues powerfully that only the infinite-personal God of Christianity answers the deepest questions and longings of lost people in our world. Intermediate.

David A. Seamands, *Healing of Memories* (Wheaton, Ill.: Victor, 1988). A Methodist pastor and seminary professor gives practical advice on how to heal a distorted emotional concept of God. Beginning.

A. W. Tozer, *The Knowledge of the Holy* (San Francisco, Calif.: Harper & Row, 1961). This classic work is a challenging and inspiring meditation on twenty of God's attributes. Intermediate.

CHAPTER FOUR

REVELATION:
GOD'S VARIOUS WAYS OF SPEAKING

"WHAT DO PEOPLE MEAN WHEN THEY SAY THE BIBLE IS 'GOD'S Word'?" I asked. Then I paused and looked across the table at the minister, who just smiled and waited for me to continue. I was a sophomore in college and had recently opened my heart to Christ.

"In the last few months I've occasionally had the experience where the Bible's words just seemed to jump off the page at me. It was as if God was speaking directly to me. Is that why people say the Bible is 'God's Word'?"

"Yes, partly," said Rev. James Hardesty.[1]

"But most of the time when I read the Bible," I continued, "it is just words on a page. Often I don't understand what I'm reading. Or at least I don't see what it has to do with me."

I paused and took a sip of coffee. "So it seems like the Bible is 'God's Word' when God uses it to speak to an individual. But the rest of the time, it's just an ordinary book made of paper and ink."

My host turned and looked at his other dinner guest,

Dr. Ronald Miller, a Bible translator who was enjoying a bite of coffee cake. Dr. Miller swallowed and smiled.

"Sounds like Alan has been reading Karl Barth."

"Carl Bart?" I said with a grin. "A guy with two first names? Sorry, never heard of him."

Jim Hardesty chuckled. "Barth[2] was a German theologian who began a movement that came to be called 'neo-orthodoxy.' He taught that the Bible is not 'God's Word' if it is sitting gathering dust on a shelf. Rather, he believed that the Bible *becomes* God's Word when God Himself speaks to us through it."

Dr. Miller looked at his friend and said, "It looks like Alan here has spontaneously reinvented neo-orthodoxy!"

I smiled but wasn't entirely sure whether I was being complimented or kidded. That dinner conversation began my thirty-year quest to understand the ways God speaks to us. Let me share with you some of what I have discovered.

GOD'S VARIOUS WAYS OF SPEAKING

Most Christian theologians use the word "revelation" as the most comprehensive term for all the ways God has shown Himself. But that leads to a critical question: "How does God reveal Himself to us?"

In Encounter or in Propositions?

As I discovered that night, a popular view among twentieth-century theologians has been that God speaks to us primarily, or some would say exclusively, in personal, subjective encounters. According to these teachers, the Bible was not written to give us information about God. Rather, the Bible was written by people who had experienced God personally. As we read their words, we too can have a personal, subjective encounter with Him.[3]

However, many current evangelicals argue that the Bible is a "propositional revelation." A proposition is simply any statement about which it is meaningful to ask the question "Is the statement true or false?" Most of the things we hear and read are in the form of propositions. Consider the statement "Alan Scholes has brown hair." That statement is a proposition because it might be true or false (as it happens, it is true). Or consider another statement: "I think that sunset is beautiful." This statement is also a proposition. Even though it is a statement about my subjective opinion, it can still be objectively true or false. Maybe I actually think the sunset rather plain, but I do not wish to contradict my friend who has just said how pretty it is. So, I could be lying.

On the other hand, some statements are not propositional. What if I just gaze at the sunset and say, "Wow!" I may in some way have expressed my feelings, but as it stands, "wow" is neither true nor false. Thus, the statement is not a proposition. Or I may say, "Jan, come here and look at this sunset!" Again, a command or imperative statement is neither true nor false and is therefore nonpropositional.

There is no question that the Bible contains statements phrased in the form of propositions. When the Bible asserts that "in the beginning, God created" or "Christ was raised on the third day," the statements are phrased in the grammatical form of propositions. What Barth and other neo-orthodox and existential theologians are arguing is not that the Bible does not contain propositional phrases. Rather, they do not believe that truth is revealed in the form of propositions. God reveals Himself to us in a personal encounter that is subjective and emotional. What words we are reading at the time the encounter occurs is largely beside the point.[4]

So who is right: the Barthian who says that revelation is personal and subjective, or the evangelical who argues that it is propositional and objective? My answer is that both are right. Perhaps a personal illustration will help clarify what I mean.

This past summer I had the privilege of teaching a theology course in the eastern European country of Croatia. Through the kind assistance of Domagoj Malovic, a Croatian national staff member with Campus Crusade for Christ, I was able to correspond with my wife in California each day via e-mail. In a place where international phone calls were unreliable and expensive, these daily letters became the lifeblood of our relationship. Daily I checked my e-mail several times, just in case she had sent me another message. In her letters, Jan often told about mundane affairs: the weather, news of our children, and how she spent her days. However, what meant the most to me were the parts that let me touch her heart—when she spoke of loneliness, discouragement, hope for the future, or her love for me. If you have ever loved another person, you will understand what I mean. It was when I caught a glimpse of her heart that she most revealed herself to me. It would not be an exaggeration to say that, at times, I encountered her through her letters.

At this point, I need to make a crucial observation. Nearly every line of every letter was phrased in the form of propositions. Even the "I love you" at the end of the letter was a proposition. (Fortunately, I have no doubt it was—and is—a true proposition!) Let us consider for a moment how I would have felt if every day she sent me an e-mail message containing no words—a completely blank page. This would have been wholly inadequate and quite frustrating. The words and propositions were essential because it was only through them that I could find out what she was doing, thinking, and feeling. My personal encounter with Jan that summer came through her propositional statements and could not have taken place without them.

Someone has suggested that the Bible is God's love letter to us. I like that analogy. Through the Bible we find out what God has done, what He thinks, and what He feels. God can speak personally to us, and we can develop a love relationship with Him. We grow to enjoy our relationship with God as we learn who He is through the words (mostly in the form of propositions) He has written to us.

So, does God speak to us in a subjective, personal encounter or through objective propositions? My answer is "Both." Often my encounters with God begin as I read and grasp the personal significance of the propositional statements written in the Bible.[5]

In General or in Special Revelation?

"Everything you could ever need or want to know is found in this book!" The preacher raised a large black Bible above his head. "You don't need school books, you don't need science books, and you certainly don't need psychology books. All you really need and all you should ever want is found right here."

I sat in the auditorium and wondered, *Could this possibly be true?* I was in my junior year of college and had been a Christian less than a year. Was everything I had learned in elementary school through college a waste of time? Should I drop out now and just read the Bible? Or maybe transfer to a Bible school? Even as a new Christian, I knew that something the preacher said didn't make sense. What about the many math classes I had taken through the years? I was pretty sure the Bible didn't contain the multiplication tables, much less a detailed explanation of solid geometry. How about language? How could I have ever read and understood the Bible if someone had not first taught me to read?

Most theologians believe God has revealed Himself in many forms other than just the Bible. Most divide the ways God has spoken into two broad categories, general and special revelation. General revelation includes what has been available to all people in all times. The Bible itself indicates at least three types of general revelation: nature,[6] God's providential dealings with the human race,[7] and moral conscience.[8] In other words, we can discover many things about God even without the Bible. Paul said these include "His invisible attributes, His eternal power, and divine nature."[9]

God also has revealed Himself in special, or specific, ways to individuals or groups at particular times and places. He used various means including dreams,[10] angels,[11] and prophets.[12] A primary way in which God has revealed Himself is through Jesus Christ.[13] Christ revealed the Father in His person,[14] His words,[15] and His deeds.[16]

The Bible itself is probably the most complete and most widely accessible form of special revelation. While other special revelations were readily available only to a few people in particular times, the Bible, through translation and copying, can potentially be made available to anyone.

Knowing the Artist Himself

In my teen years, before I came to Christ, one of my favorite things was to drive over the hills that separated my town of Los Altos from the ocean. Especially in winter, I loved to drive to the coastal village of Half Moon Bay. The beaches were usually deserted, and all alone I would walk along the shore or stand on a rocky point as waves engulfed my ankles.

In those days I told people, "I feel closer to God at the beach than I do in any church." In a sense, I was experiencing God, at least indirectly. Through the rugged rocks and crashing waves He had made, I sensed something of His beauty and awesome power. These were, I believe, genuine experiences of general revelation. But I knew little or nothing about my own sin, God's plan for me, or the purpose of Christ's death on the cross.[17] That knowledge came initially through the testimony of Christians and soon from my own reading of the Bible.

As a teen, my relationship with God through nature was like admiring an artist's painting in a gallery. Now my time with Him is more like sitting down with an artist over a cup of coffee and talking at length about his art as well as about our mutual joys and sorrows and our hopes and dreams. My connection with God used to be remote, indirect, and ultimately impersonal. Now, through the Bible, it can be immediate, intimate, and personal.

In the next chapter we will continue to look at the Bible. We will try to understand more about how God speaks to us through the Bible and how we can trust everything He says to us through it.

■ FOR PERSONAL REFLECTION ■

1. Who do you think is right: the Barthian who says that revelation is personal and subjective or the evangelical who argues that it is propositional and objective?
2. What difference is your answer to question 1 going to make in the kind of relationship you have with God?
3. Do you think God has revealed enough in nature for a person to be saved without ever seeing a Bible or speaking to a Christian? Why or why not?
4. What would you say to someone who says, "I feel closer to God at the beach than I do in any church"?

■ GROUP DISCUSSION GUIDE ■

1. Group project: Divide the group (or class) into two discussion groups. Have one subgroup discuss the question "How would your own relationship with God be different if you did not believe the Bible contained propositional revelation?" Have the other group discuss "How would your own relationship with God be different if you never experienced personal, subjective encounters with Him (if your only connection with God was through propositions in the Bible)?" After ten to fifteen minutes, have each group report briefly to the others.
2. What are some answers we might give to someone who says, "Religion is a very private matter. I don't think it's good to discuss it with other people."
3. What are some benefits to you personally of discussing God and your relationship in a group such as this?

■ RECOMMENDED READING ■

Paul Enns, *The Moody Handbook of Theology* (Chicago: Moody, 1989). This excellent overall resource contains short summaries of neo-orthodox theology and evangelical bibliology. Intermediate.

Millard J. Erickson, *Christian Theology* (Grand Rapids, Mich.: Baker, 1983–1985). Baptist systematic theologian Erickson has excellent chapters on "Theology and Its Language" as well as general and special revelation. This is one of the most readable and devotional of the in-depth systematic theologies. Intermediate-advanced.

Millard J. Erickson, *Postmodernizing the Faith: Evangelical Responses to the Challenge of Postmodernism* (Grand Rapids, Mich.: Baker, 1998). Erickson gives a thoughtful and critical examination of evangelicals who are embracing aspects of postmodernism. Intermediate.

Os Guinness, *Fit Bodies, Fat Minds: Why Evangelicals Don't Think and What to Do About It* (Grand Rapids, Mich.: Baker, 1994). Sociologist Guinness gives a devastating critique of the anti-intellectualism in American society in general and in evangelicalism in particular. Beginning.

David L. Smith, *A Handbook of Contemporary Theology* (Wheaton, Ill.: Victor, 1992). In a fourteen-page chapter, Smith gives a good summary of Barth and neo-orthodoxy from an evangelical perspective. The volume also includes helpful chapters on post-Vatican II Catholicism, Eastern Orthodoxy, process theology, theologies of success, and reconstructionist theology, among others. Intermediate.

CHAPTER FIVE

THE BIBLE: GOD'S SPECIAL WAY OF SPEAKING

JIM WORE A WORRIED FROWN. "I DID THE READING YOU assigned, but now I'm more confused than when I started!" Though Jim was a new believer, he was one of the sharpest students in my graduate theology class.

"What exactly has you confused?" I asked.

"It's all these words I've been reading about the Bible: *infallible, inerrant, inspired, reliable*. . . .Why can't we just say that it's true and be done with it?"

INSPIRATION: WHAT THE BIBLE TEACHES ABOUT ITSELF

Jim's question is a good one. The terminology surrounding current discussions about the Bible can be daunting. Part of the difficulty is the particular time in which we live. Until about two hundred years ago, the exact nature of the Bible and its truthfulness wasn't seriously debated within Christendom. Nonbelievers attacked the Bible, of course, but little was written by Christian theologians trying to define the nature of the

Scriptures. As someone has said, "For the first eighteen hundred years, the church debated every doctrine in the Bible, but not the doctrine of the Bible itself." But now, in our era of church history, theologians are working to develop a clearer understanding of the Bible's nature. In other words: What terminology is most appropriate to describe the Bible itself?

Is It Inspired?

"Inspiration" is probably the most central and widely used term for the supernatural quality of the Bible. Paul affirmed that "all Scripture is inspired by God."[1] The Greek text says literally that the Bible is "God-breathed." But what, exactly, does it mean to say the Bible is inspired or God-breathed?

Although the Bible does not give us a complete description of how God inspired Scripture, one important clue is found in the second of Peter's letters. He said there that Old Testament prophets did not speak words that originated solely in their own human will but rather "men moved by the Holy Spirit spoke from God."[2] This is the clearest biblical picture we have of the process of inspiration. The original Greek gives the picture of someone being picked up and carried along for a period of time.

Apparently the Holy Spirit was the agent of inspiration.[3] Paul declared, "The Holy Spirit rightly spoke through Isaiah the prophet to your fathers."[4] When an earthly author spoke for God in Scripture, it is equally appropriate to attribute the words to the human author or to God. On two different occasions, Jesus quoted Exodus 20:12; on one occasion He introduced the quotation by declaring, "Moses said . . ."[5] and on the other by stating that "God said . . ."[6] Both are true! They were Moses' words and also God the Holy Spirit's words. It is passages like these that lead most evangelical theologians to reject the idea that the human authors were merely passive scribes, dutifully copying down God's words (the dictation theory).[7] Rather, God the Holy Spirit worked in a partnership with His chosen human authors, using their thoughts, words, and writing styles to express what He desired.

How About "Infallible"?

The result of the human/divine partnership is the infallible Word of God. The word "infallible" means "does not or cannot fail." The natural question to ask at this point would be "Does not fail to do *what?*" The answer would be that the Bible does not fail in giving us guidance and communicating those things that God desires to communicate.[8] In recent years, however, this term "infallible" has become part of a controversy within evangelicalism. To understand this controversy, it will help if we take a brief trip back in time.

First, let's consider what "infallible" used to mean. During the last century, the term was employed by defenders of the Bible like Hodge and Warfield at Princeton Seminary. At that time (and still today), some liberal theologians argued that because fallible, finite humans actually penned the Bible, the result could not help but be fallible. Hodge and Warfield countered that the Holy Spirit had superintended the process of writing so that the result was infallible.[9] So, for much of the twentieth century, evangelicals used the word "infallible" to mean that the Bible can be trusted to be completely true in any area where it speaks to us. It will not fail to tell us the truth.

However, beginning in the 1960s, some evangelicals began to teach that the Bible might be infallible but still contain some kinds of errors. A number of the faculty at Fuller Seminary in Pasadena, California, began to believe and teach this view.[10] These faculty members, including Daniel Fuller, the son of the seminary's founder, faced a dilemma. The seminary's statement of faith, which all faculty were required to sign each year, not only affirmed that the Bible is "the only infallible rule of faith and practice" but also stated that it was "free from all error."

These teachers were comfortable with the "infallible" clause because they understood the word "faith" to mean doctrine and "practice" to refer to moral teaching. They continued to believe that the Bible could be trusted to guide us in matters of morality and theology. But they believed it contained errors of science, history, chronology, and other "minor" areas, and consequently they were no longer comfortable with the phrase "free from all error." Eventually, with the cooperation of the trustees and the president of the seminary, in 1972 the statement was changed. The new statement retained the ideas of inspiration and infallibility but deleted the phrases that affirmed inerrancy. The new statement now reads, "All the books of the Old and New Testaments, given by divine inspiration, are the written word of God, the only infallible rule of faith and practice." The new Fuller statement began a trend among certain evangelicals of believing in "infallibility" but not trusting the Bible in all matters on which it speaks.

Inerrant, Too?

Can we say, with confidence, not only that the Bible will not fail to properly guide us in matters of faith and practice but also that it is totally without error of any sort? Can a rational person believe that the Bible is totally true when it speaks on any subject, not just religious ones?

Before I answer that question, I would like to clarify a few points. First, both inerrantists and those who hold the only-infallible-in-matters-of-faith-and-practice view agree that we are only talking about the original manuscripts of the Bible, the texts as they were originally penned by the human authors. I know of no evangelical scholar today who claims inerrancy (or infallibility) for any modern copy. So what the "only infallible" advocates are claiming is not that some incidental errors have crept in during the process of centuries of copying manuscripts. Rather, they believe that these inconsistencies were in the original manuscripts.

Second, those who hold the "only infallible" view are not saying (as many liberals do) that God could not have superintended the human authors to prevent the occurrence of error of any sort. They are already affirming that God the Holy Spirit prevented any errors in matters of faith and practice. Rather, they charge that those who insist on inerrancy are applying a modern notion of accuracy in things like science and history to works that God chose originally to reveal in cultures that were much less concerned with such things.

For me, this is the crux of the question. If the inerrantists are simply a bunch of fussy nitpickers who insist that the Bible must speak in a manner consistent with some arbitrarily modern scientific (or even American) idea of precision, then I would agree that Fuller was right in deleting the idea of "free from error" from its statement. So the whole question turns on what the first-century believers (particularly Jesus and His apostles) thought of the Bible. I do not believe that we should demand more "precision" from it than they did.

The primary reason I believe that the Bible is inerrant (as well as infallible) is that "free from error" seems to me to be a very good description of Jesus' (and His early followers') view of Scripture. Jesus asserted that "the Scripture cannot be broken."[11] He declared that "until heaven and earth pass away, not the smallest letter or stroke shall pass away from the Law."[12] Further, Jesus taught in a manner that seems very much like the modern inerrantist view, using the Bible to prove His points. He quoted the Old Testament, "I AM THE GOD OF ABRAHAM"[13] and concluded from the present tense of the verb that Abraham was still alive, for otherwise God would have said, "I *was* the God of Abraham"! Jesus based a theological conclusion (resurrection) on the tense of a verb. For Jesus, inspiration must have extended to the words and even the tenses.

Someone who holds the Fuller view might object to my use of this passage by saying that Jesus was trying to argue a point of doctrine (the resurrection of the dead), which is a matter of faith. Maybe Jesus only trusted the Old Testament when it was teaching doctrine or morals. It is a fair point. Let me answer it with another example from Jesus' teaching. Jesus predicted His own death and resurrection by quoting from Jonah. "For just as JONAH WAS THREE DAYS AND THREE NIGHTS IN THE BELLY OF THE SEA MONSTER, so shall the Son of Man be three days and three nights in the heart of the earth."[14] One of the common problems raised by those who question inerrancy is the issue of whether Jesus could have been crucified on Friday and raised on Sunday and still have been in the grave for three twenty-four-hour periods.[15] There is no question that Jesus was teaching doctrine in this verse. Does it make sense to say, "Jesus only meant Jonah's experience as a prophetic prefigurement of what would happen to Him—He did not mean to teach anything about the three days and nights being prophetic"? My question is: Why, then, did Jesus mention the three days and nights, both in reference to Jonah and Himself? It would have been a simple matter for Jesus to simply say, "As Jonah returned from the belly of the monster, so I will return from the heart of the earth."

The point I'm trying to make is that I do not think we can second-guess Jesus or any of the biblical writers and accurately decide what is doctrine and what is incidental chronological detail (and therefore potentially errant). Jesus made a point of the three days and nights. Therefore, I think we must regard it as an integral part of His teaching.

I sympathize with Jim, the graduate student, who was confused by all the terms. The terms are confusing! Charles Ryrie summarized the frustrating evolution of our modern terminology.

> Not many years ago all one had to say to affirm his belief in the full inspiration of the Bible was that he believed it was "the Word of God." Then it became necessary to add "the inspired Word of God." Later he had to include "the verbally, inspired Word of God." Then to mean the same thing he had to say "the plenary (fully), verbally, inspired Word of God." Today one has to say "the plenary, verbally, infallible, inspired, and inerrant-in-the-original manuscripts Word of God." And even then, he may not communicate clearly![16]

But despite the risk of jargon overload I may be creating, I need to discuss one more term. It is probably the most important aspect of the trustworthiness of the Bible.

Definitely Authoritative?

Authority has become an increasingly unpopular concept in Western society. We distrust our political leaders, our parents, the police, the legal system, large corporations—in short, any and all of those who wield authority. However, I think it's crucial to remember that we do not merely distrust authority *per se;* rather, we're often suspicious of it because so many people in authority have failed to behave in a manner worthy of our trust.

Yet when Jesus spoke, people listened and were amazed because "He was teaching them as one having authority, and not as their scribes."[17] The religious leaders of Jesus' day didn't deserve the trust of the people and did not receive it. But many recognized in Jesus something truly worthy of their trust. Jesus passed this authority on to His disciples. Even the Jewish high council "observed the confidence of Peter and John . . . and began to recognize them as having been with Jesus."[18]

Someone has rightly observed, "If you stand for nothing, you'll fall for anything." We in the West at the beginning of the twenty-first century like to see ourselves as independent and self-reliant, making our own decisions without the need of any authority to tell us what to do. Even many who call themselves Christians are reluctant to place their minds and hearts fully under the authority of Christ and His Word. We are afraid that we will become mindless, undiscerning robots. Actually, the reverse is true.

The cults and groups practicing Eastern mysticism are exploding. The repackaged spiritualism of the new age movement is a growing cultural influence. "Pagan" has again become a positive label in some circles. Why, in our enlightened, objective, scientific age, do intelligent, educated people fall for such nonsense? Because if you remove yourself from the one truly trustworthy authority in the universe, you become like a ship cut loose from its moorings in the midst of a hurricane. Reveling in your independence, you are blown out of control toward inevitable moral, spiritual, and intellectual shipwreck.[19]

I believe that affirming the authority of the Bible is a crucial difference between Christian and nonbeliever, between Christian and cultist, between evangelical and liberal. Therefore, I believe the authority of Scripture should be held at a conviction level of belief.[20]

CANONICITY: WHICH BOOKS ARE "SCRIPTURE"?

"How can you trust anything in the Bible?" The red-haired young woman leaned back in her chair as she spoke. "A bunch of old white males got together in the third century and decided which books to include in the Bible. How do we know they made the right decisions? Maybe they simply tacked up a list of all the early writings and threw darts at it! Or, more likely, they chose the ones that agreed with their prejudices and would silence their enemies!"

The question is not an idle one. All the discussion over inspiration and inerrancy becomes moot if the books in the Bible might not be the ones God inspired. However, the red-haired woman's picture of how we got our canon of Scripture is quite distorted.[21]

What Was the Process?

The process actually included these three stringent "tests for canonicity":

1. Authority of the writer. This test asked if the human writer of the book was in a position of recognized authority as a legitimate carrier of God's message. In the case of the New Testament writings, these early church leaders wanted to be sure the writer was an apostle or a close associate of an apostle. They immediately rejected any book written after the apostolic era. We should remember that believers in the fourth century may well have had information about these writers that we no longer possess.

2. Edifying content. The early leaders wanted to be satisfied that the book reflected the sort of high moral and spiritual values that demonstrate a work of the Holy Spirit. They considered whether a book's teachings were consistent with accepted orthodoxy. They considered whether many believers had a sense of blessing and guidance when they read the book in question.

3. Widespread acceptance. The councils selected only those books that were already widely accepted by the early church as a whole. Many of the rejected books were written by Gnostics or other heretical teachers in an attempt to promote their own theological agendas.

When Was the Canon Formed?

With regard to our Old Testament, Jewish tradition names the biblical figure Ezra as the first one who collected all of the Old Testament books. By the time of Jesus, the Jewish community accepted as "the Scriptures" the books we now list as the Old Testament.[22]

When it comes to the New Testament, we believe that in A.D. 367 Athanasius, the bishop of Alexandria, Egypt, was the first to publish a list of all the New Testament books. There followed a series of church councils to consider the question of canonicity, ending with the Council of Carthage in 397, which endorsed the canon we have today.

It is crucial to realize that these councils did not *create* the canon. The canon was created when God inspired the books. All of these books were widely recognized and accepted by the early church during the first four centuries. The lists were merely formalized by the councils. One of their prime motivations was to refute the claims of heretics who were pushing for some of their own books to be added to those already widely accepted. As René Pache comments:

It was not a matter of councils, either Jewish or Christian, imposing on the church books first thought of as human, which they later, by some sort of decree, lifted up to what they claimed to be a divine level. Quite the contrary: works born out of supernatural inspiration, through the silent work of the Holy Spirit, were made acceptable to the whole Christian community. In fact, . . . Scripture antedated the church and furnished its foundation, framework, doctrine and spiritual strength. Practically all the apostolic writings were recognized by the great majority of believers before the Nicean Council in 325.[23]

After I had known the Lord for about a year, the question of the canon began to bother me. So I went to my secular college library and found a book that contained some of the writings the councils had rejected.[24] To that point I had read through the New Testament only once. However, the difference between the rejected books and the authentic Scriptures was obvious. Many of the books rambled and were repetitive. Others painted an entirely different picture of Jesus from the one I'd seen in the four Gospels. Though I was still a young Christian, it was not hard for me to see why the early councils rejected these books.

Do We Have Accurate Copies?

The final question we need to consider is whether the copies of the Bible we have today are accurate reproductions of the original manuscripts. This is what theologians call the issue of reliability. I mentioned earlier that evangelical scholars claim infallibility for only the first edition of each book as it came from the hand of the biblical writer (called the "autograph"). Until the invention of the printing press and the first printed Bible in 1456, all copies of the Bible were made laboriously by hand. With all those centuries of copying, couldn't some errors have crept in? The answer is there could, and there were, errors made in the copying process. The evangelical position is not that our modern Greek and Hebrew texts of the Bible contain no copyist errors. Rather, we point out that in this century, the science of manuscript evidence has progressed to the point where we can trust the integrity and reliability of our modern biblical texts.[25]

Many have written about the details of these issues, and I do not wish to repeat these excellent treatments here.[26] But the conclusion of centuries of collecting, sorting, and preserving is important. We can have great confidence that the Bible we hold today is an excellent, reliable copy of the original. The variants are primarily in spelling and grammar, and none of them affect any doctrinal or moral teaching. The fact that there are a few minor differences in ancient manuscripts does not undermine my confidence in the inerrancy of the original autographs or my trust in the Bible I hold in my hands.

A few years ago, I spoke to teacher convocations in two cities in Siberia, Russia. My topic was the evidence for the reliability of Scripture, a perspective none of them had ever heard. As public school teachers, they had all received Soviet-era indoctrination courses in "scientific atheism." My airplane flight from California to Russia happened to include an overnight in London. I hurried from the plane to the Underground, which took me to the British Museum. With only an hour until closing time, I rushed through the many cavernous halls until I found what I sought. There, in a rather unimpressive glass case, lay *Codex Sinaiticus,* the oldest existing complete manuscript of the New Testament. The copy was made in the early fourth century, just a little more than two hundred years after the completion of the New Testament writings.[27] A few days later I stood before hundreds of Russian teachers. I told them I had seen with my own eyes a very early copy of the Bible that scholars tell us varies hardly at all from the Russian Bibles we were giving them as a part of the conference.

Come Again?

In case you are like my graduate student Jim and still are a bit unclear about all the nomenclature used in referring to the Bible, let me close this chapter by giving a concise definition for each of the terms we've discussed.

Inspired: Made up of words given by the Holy Spirit in partnership with human authors.

Infallible: Does not fail us. (Fuller Seminary view: Does not fail in matters of faith and practice.)

Inerrant: Free from error in any subject on which it speaks.

Authoritative: Deserves the submission of our hearts and minds.

Canonical: Chosen by God to be included in the Scriptures.

Reliable: Trustworthy as a copy. The existing manuscripts are highly accurate copies of the originals.

One of the primary ways we come to know and enjoy God is by listening to Him speak to us through His Word, the Bible. Our minds can rest with confidence because the evidence for its truthfulness is overwhelming. Our hearts can freely embrace what He tells us there as nourishment for our whole person. We can do as Peter encouraged us and "like newborn babes, long for the pure milk of the word, that by it you may grow."[28]

■ FOR PERSONAL REFLECTION ■

1. List the central points of disagreement between those who think the Bible is merely "infallible in matters of faith and practice" and those who believe it is inerrant. Which view do you think is right? Why?

2. Do you agree that the authority of the Bible is a conviction-level belief but that inerrancy should be held only at the

persuasion level? (see note #20, page 199) Why or why not?
3. Do you have any doubts about whether we have the right books in our Bible? If so, how would you go about resolving those doubts?
4. How can we trust the Bible we have today, considering we do not possess any of the original manuscripts (autographs)?
5. Can you completely trust the Bible you own to be God's own words spoken to you? Why or why not? If you have any doubts, how could they be resolved?

■ GROUP DISCUSSION GUIDE ■

1. Debate: Choose two members (best to recruit before meeting) to debate the importance of inerrancy. Assign one to argue that it is crucial for Christians to believe that the Bible is true even in matters of history, geography, chronology, and so on. Have the other argue that it is enough to believe that the Bible can be trusted in matters of doctrine and morals and that we shouldn't nitpick over details.
2. What arguments might someone put forward for assigning inerrancy to the conviction level? What arguments are there for considering it a persuasion-level belief? Which arguments are strongest?
3. Are there any objections to or problems in the Bible that any of you have found personally confusing (or hard to answer when others bring them up)? What might be some possible answers or approaches to those problems?

RECOMMENDED READING

Norman L. Geisler, *Inerrancy* (Grand Rapids, Mich.: Zondervan, 1979). This collection of fourteen papers originally delivered to the International Conference on Biblical

Inerrancy (Chicago, 1978) also contains "The Chicago Statement on Biblical Inerrancy" signed by the participants. Contributors include J. Barton Payne, Walter Kaiser, Jr., J. I. Packer, Gordon Lewis, Paul Feinberg, R. C. Sproul, and John Gerstner. Intermediate-advanced.

Harold Lindsell, *The Battle for the Bible* (Grand Rapids, Mich.: Zondervan, 1976). Lindsell, one of the founding faculty members at Fuller argues both historically and biblically for inerrancy. This book single-handedly ignited the American inerrancy controversy of the 1970s and 1980s and led to the reforming of the Southern Baptist Conference and the Missouri Synod Lutheran Church. Intermediate.

Tremper Longman III, *Reading the Bible with Heart and Mind* (Colorado Springs, Colo.: NavPress, 1997). An Old Testament professor at Westmont College challenges and gives practical tips on how to read God's Word for life change. Beginning-intermediate.

Josh McDowell, *Evidence That Demands a Verdict* (San Bernardino, Calif.: Campus Crusade for Christ, 1972). McDowell, a speaker for Campus Crusade for Christ, pulls together a large body of research presented in outline form. It includes particularly helpful chapters on canonicity and transmission. Intermediate.

René Pache, *The Inspiration and Authority of Scripture* (Chicago: Moody, 1969). Written by a European evangelical, this readable volume includes excellent discussions of inspiration, canonicity, transmission, and authority. Pache defends inerrancy. Intermediate.

Jack Rogers, ed., *Biblical Authority* (Waco, Tex.: Word, 1977). This collection of essays edited by a Fuller professor defends the "infallible in faith and practice" view. A response to Lindsell's *Battle for the Bible,* it includes chapters by Rogers, Clark Pinnock, Bernard Ramm, and David Hubbard. Intermediate.

CHAPTER SIX

CHRIST:
THE MAN WHO IS GOD

MY EARLIEST IMAGES OF JESUS WERE FORMED BY MOVIES. The first time I saw Christ portrayed on screen, Jeffrey Hunter was playing the lead role in the Hollywood extravaganza *King of Kings*. Hunter's blue eyes and conventional leading-man good looks seemed just right for Jesus when I was fourteen. A few years later I was startled to see Max von Sydow's interpretation in *The Greatest Story Ever Told*. Sydow's Christ was gaunt, almost emaciated, and never smiled. The *Gospel According to St. Matthew* showed a Jesus constantly in motion, a radical who cut across the grain of first-century society. The decade of the 1970s offered two musical interpretations of Jesus. *Jesus Christ Superstar* reinterpreted Jesus as a first-century rock idol. *Godspell,* while more reverent, added little to my picture of Christ.[1] The 1979 production of *Jesus* cast Brian Deacon in an authentic, almost documentary, portrayal of Christ that was refreshing after the glitz of so many of Hollywood's efforts.

My favorite movie portrayal of Jesus may seem, at first, an odd one. In the movie *Ben Hur* (subtitled *A Story of the Christ*), Jesus appears in only a few scenes, and we never see His face. Among the many memorable scenes in this classic film, one particularly moves me. It's the scene that shows Judah Ben Hur as a prisoner in a slave caravan that stops for water in the dusty town of Nazareth. By order, Ben Hur has been denied water.

But then a robed figure, whom we see only from the waist down, stoops and raises a gourd filled with life-giving water to the prisoner's lips. A brutish Roman legionary shouts, "I said no water for him!" The Roman moves to stop the kneeling figure . . . and their eyes meet. We see only the hardened face of the soldier as the look on it changes from fierce anger to uncertainty. Then we catch a glimpse of cowed fear as he turns away. For me those two looks—the first of awe and gratitude by Charlton Heston (playing Ben Hur) as he receives the drink, and the second by the uncredited Italian actor who played the legionary—touched me more deeply than all of the other movies about Christ combined.

Who is Jesus? I learned early that I would find no consistent answer in a darkened theater.

THE GOD WHO BECAME MAN

Danish philosopher and theologian Søren Kierkegaard declared that the idea of God becoming a man was logically incomprehensible. He called it the "Absolute Paradox."[2] He said it could only be believed by a "leap of faith." My own experience is that many have rejected Christianity because they found the Incarnation unintelligible, simply unworthy of being taken seriously by a modern, educated person. However, as a Christian who accepts the Bible as God's propositional, inerrant communication, I find compelling reasons to believe this teaching.[3] As we will see in this chapter, the Bible clearly teaches both that Christ is fully God and that He became fully human.

Faced with the clear biblical teaching, must we, with Kierkegaard, simply throw up our hands and say, "It seems like nonsense, so we'll just accept it by faith and not try to understand it"? I think there is a better response. As mentioned earlier in this book, Jesus said that we should worship God with our minds (among other ways).[4] God is not (as some Eastern religions and Western cults teach) above and beyond rational thinking. Rather, His rationality is the source of our ability to reason and understand. Yet our limited reason is a dim reflection of His infinitely rational mind. I cannot assume I currently am equipped to grasp everything that God is and does and knows; that would be arrogant. Jesus once told His disciples that He had much more He wanted to tell them that they were not yet ready to handle.[5] I have no doubt that Jesus feels the same way about me today. Because of my immaturity, my indifference, or simply my finitude, there will always be more He wishes to tell me than I am ready to grasp.[6]

What, then, would be a balanced response to difficult teachings like the two natures of Christ (that He is fully God and fully human)? I believe God wants us to strive to understand such things as completely as we can but recognize that our viewpoint is finite, our knowledge incomplete, and our minds clouded by sin.

He Is Fully God

In nearly thirty years of speaking, teaching, and counseling with university students around the world, I have rarely had a student doubt that Jesus was fully and completely human. Nearly all the questions and objections about His nature have centered on the difficulty in accepting that He is fully God.

Much of the current skepticism about Jesus' deity stems from a critical school of theological and biblical scholarship that became popular in the 1800s and continues today. Responding to secular Enlightenment philosophers such as Hume and Kant, Friedrich Schleiermacher rejected the authority of Scripture and the deity of Christ, among other doctrines.[7] Soon after, a number of skeptical Bible scholars began what is known as "the search for the historical Jesus."[8]

These scholars shared several assumptions derived from Enlightenment philosophy. The most significant of these is that genuine miracles are impossible. In addition, most of these writers assumed that much of the picture we see of Jesus in the four Gospels was the invention of the early church. Consequently, from the beginning of the "search," they set out to separate the "Jesus of history" (the actual person who lived in the first century) from the "Christ of faith" (the mythological miracle worker invented by the early church).

In recent years the two-hundred-year-old assumptions of the "search" have resurfaced in the Jesus Seminar under the leadership of its founder, Robert Funk. What is new about the Seminar is not the assumptions of its scholars but the way their conclusions have been popularized.[9] In the Seminar's controversial book, *The Five Gospels,* a group of predominantly liberal scholars "rate" the sayings of Jesus found in the four canonical Gospels and also those found in the apocryphal gospel of Thomas.[10] For each of the supposed sayings of Jesus, scholars "voted" by placing colored beads in a ballot box. A red bead meant "Jesus undoubtedly said this or something very like it." A pink one indicated that "Jesus probably said something like this." Gray meant "Jesus did not say this, but the ideas contained are close to His own." Black beads were reserved for "Jesus did not say this; it represents the perspective or content of a later or different tradition."[11]

What were the results when the votes were tallied? According to these scholars, only 18 percent of Jesus' words in the four Gospels were actually spoken by Him. Not surprisingly, they eliminated all of the gospel of John.[12] What is more surprising is that the Seminar's scholars were confident about only one of Jesus' sayings recorded in Mark.[13] Most scholars, even those who share many of the Seminar's assumptions, view Mark as the earliest of the four Gospels. Incredibly, the gospel of Thomas, which nearly all scholars view as a later Gnostic creation, scored higher than Mark and John. Three of Jesus' sayings in Thomas garnered the red color. Yet here are some of Jesus' rejected words: "Whoever wishes to save his life shall lose it; and whoever loses his life for My sake and the gospel's shall save it."[14] Sorry, the Seminar scholars are certain Jesus never said it. As for "Every tree that does not bear good fruit is cut down and thrown into the fire,"[15] later Christians invented that one!

Nearly all the sayings in John's gospel got the dreaded black bead. Among them are the following:

- "You must be born again."[16]
- "For God so loved the world. . . ."[17]
- "God is spirit; and those who worship Him must worship in spirit and truth."[18]
- "I am the bread of life."[19]
- "He who is without sin among you, let him be the first to throw a stone."[20]
- "You shall know the truth, and the truth shall make you free."[21]
- "I am the vine, you are the branches."[22]
- "This is My commandment, that you love one another, just as I have loved you."[23]
- "I am thirsty. . . . It is finished!"[24]

I hate to break the news to you. The fine scholars at the Jesus Seminar are sure Jesus never said any of those things.

But we know that Jesus was God! In chapter 5, I gave the reasons why we can trust the Bible to be not only an accurate record of what Jesus said and did, but God's inerrant Word as well.[25] By His own words and deeds, recorded in the Gospels, Jesus showed that He was God. He said He and the Father were one.[26] He claimed to be God's own Son.[27] He claimed to have the power to forgive all sin.[28] He claimed that all judgment was given to Him,[29] and that He had the power to give direction to God's Holy Spirit.[30] He even claimed that He would raise back to life those who had died.[31] Jesus proved the truth of these claims by performing many miracles,[32] including raising the dead.[33]

He Is Fully Man

Surprisingly, Christians in the first few centuries had the opposite problem of most people today. Under Gnostic influence, many people in the early years of the Christian era believed that Christ was God but not completely human.[34] And yet, while such a view is not common today, there is a danger in modern Christendom that we will unconsciously neglect or underemphasize the idea that Jesus was fully human because we're so seldom called upon to defend it. I've noticed that many Christians today mentally envision Jesus as a kind of demigod or superman who is somehow above all human problems. Because this side of the teaching is often neglected by Christians in modern times, I would like to go into the evidence for Christ's humanity in greater detail.

His body is fully human. Although we take this point for granted, one of the distinctives of being human is that we possess a human body. We can see that Jesus' body is fully human because He experienced thirst,[35] hunger,[36] sorrow that led to tears,[37] and because He became tired.[38] Perhaps the most dramatic evidence that Jesus had a real, physical, human body came when He invited the skeptical Thomas to place his finger in His nail prints and to put his hand in His wounded side.

His soul and spirit are fully human. The Bible tells us that Jesus possesses a soul[39] and a spirit.[40] Some teachers have claimed that His body is strictly human but that His soul or spirit is completely divine. Historically the church has rejected this view, and properly so. Jesus is fully human (as well as fully God) in all His aspects.[41]

So, we have good biblical reasons for believing that Christ is fully God and yet truly human at the same time. This leads us to at least two questions about God becoming man: (1) why did He become human, and (2) how did He accomplish it?

First, *why* did God become one of us? The immediate answer to the question is that in order to have a personal relationship with us, God had to come to us and He had to come to us in a way we could understand.[42] Christ also lived a perfect human life, showing us how we should live.[43] This leads us to the most important reason He became one of us, which was to die in our place and provide the sacrifice for our sin.[44] In short, Christ became one of us so that He might restore us to a relationship with God.[45]

Our second question is, *How* did God become one of us? The means God chose to become human was through the Virgin Birth of Christ. This was predicted in Isaiah 7:14, and its fulfillment is described in Matthew 1:23. Although the Bible does not explain in detail why the Virgin Birth was necessary to keep Jesus from receiving the sin nature of Adam, Luke 1:35 does assert that because of the virgin conception, Mary's offspring would be "holy."[46]

He "Emptied" Himself

Now it is time to try to answer what is undoubtedly one of the most perplexing questions in all of theology. How is it possible for the infinite God to fit inside a finite human mind and body? How is it possible for the omnipresent God to walk the hills of Galilee and to be in only one place at a time? How can the omniscient and omnipotent God be "increasing in wisdom and stature" as Luke says of Jesus?[47] In short, how is it possible for God to become man?

The clearest answer we find in Scripture comes from chapter 2 of Philippians, where Paul wrote that Christ Jesus "emptied Himself, taking the form of a bond-servant, and being made in the likeness of men" (verse 7). The exact meaning of this word "emptied" has been debated by Christian thinkers for more than sixteen hundred years. Of what, exactly, did Jesus empty Himself?

Some have suggested that the second person of the Trinity gave up His deity while on earth as Jesus. This is clearly unbiblical because, as we saw above, Jesus was God while on earth. Many modern evangelicals have argued that He only veiled His glory or added humanity to His deity. My problem with these less radical suggestions is that while they preserve the deity of Christ, they do not help answer the question of how God could live as a finite human.

The view I find most attractive (and hold at a persuasion level) is that Jesus chose voluntarily not to use His infinite attributes during His earthly life. This explains why Jesus sometimes did not know things and had other limitations that go with being human.[48] "But what about the times when Jesus prophesied the future or performed miracles?" someone might object. "Didn't He exercise His omniscience or omnipresence at those times?" My answer is that Jesus depended on the Holy Spirit for supernatural power just as His disciples did. If this view is true, it means that Jesus is our perfect example of the Spirit-filled life—He depended on the Holy Spirit just as we must.[49]

He Died and Rose Again

The death and resurrection of Christ are at the heart of the Christian gospel. We will look at Christ's death and its significance in the chapter on salvation, but here I wish to make a few comments about the resurrection of our Lord.

It has been common in twentieth-century theology to either deny or belittle the importance of the Resurrection. Many neo-orthodox and existentialist theologians have said the issue is not important. Jesus may or may not have physically risen from the tomb. What is important is the sense of optimism and the proclamation of new life that was preached by the early Christian community. It is the spiritual message of hope that is the importance of Easter for the believer, not a debate over whether Jesus' body came back to life. Other, more liberal theologians have ridiculed the doctrine of the bodily Resurrection as contrary to scientific knowledge or modern sensibility.

So, is the biblical teaching that Christ rose bodily from the grave an optional or irrelevant doctrine? Clearly the early Christians did not think so. Paul tied the entire truth of the gospel to the fact that Jesus physically rose. "If Christ has not been raised, your faith is worthless; you are still in your sins."[50] Jesus' resurrection was at the center of the apostle's evangelistic message.[51] What is behind the reluctance to talk about the Resurrection is the current antagonism to miracles that has come into our Western culture through the ideas of the Enlightenment. I have often been tempted to gloss over the subject of the Resurrection, particularly when talking to educated nonbelievers. But I have learned that we must, with the apostles, proclaim a risen Christ.[52] When I have done so, I have often been surprised that even educated, sophisticated skeptics are willing to discuss what Christ said and did. I am also finding that the current generation is much more open to ideas about the supernatural than were many of my own generation.[53]

Kierkegaard and the existentialists are right that there is much about Christ's life, death, and resurrection that goes beyond the ability of mere human reason to prove or even fully comprehend. But it is also true that many of the greatest intellects of history, including Augustine, Thomas Aquinas, Jonathan Edwards, and C. S. Lewis, to name just a few, have considered it entirely rational to believe in the Christ of the Bible. We can and should bring all that we are, including all our knowledge, and joyfully kneel at the feet of Christ in worship and love.

■ FOR PERSONAL REFLECTION ■

1. Describe how you think Jesus looked. What movies, paintings, or other representations of Christ have influenced your picture of Him?
2. Do you think it is irrational to believe Jesus is both fully God and fully man? Why or why not?

3. How would you respond to someone who had read about, and was influenced by, the Jesus Seminar?
4. When you think of Jesus Christ, does your mental image of Him emphasize His humanity or His deity? Why do you lean the way you do in your image of Him?
5. Why is it important to believe and preach the resurrection of Christ?

■ GROUP DISCUSSION GUIDE ■

1. Picture project: Have all the group members write a brief description or draw a picture of what they think Jesus looks like. Have each read (or show) his or her picture and tell what movies, drawings, or other things influenced his or her image of Him.
2. Which is harder for you: to think of Jesus as God, or to think of Him as an actual man? Why do you think one is harder for you than the other?
3. Do you agree that Jesus' "emptying Himself" means that He voluntarily gave up the use of His infinite attributes during His earthly life? Why do you agree or disagree?
4. What are some practical ways that we can feel closer to Christ and walk more intimately with Him? Are there specific ways this group of believers could help each of us grow closer to Him?

■ RECOMMENDED READING ■

Stephen T. Davis, *Risen Indeed: Making Sense of the Resurrection* (Grand Rapids, Mich.: Eerdmans, 1993). Evangelical philosopher of religion Davis gives convincing arguments for the intellectual credibility of belief in Christ's resurrection. Intermediate.

Robert W. Funk, Roy W. Hoover, and the Jesus Seminar, *The Five Gospels: The Search for the Authentic Words of Jesus*

(New York: Macmillan, 1993). Nothing will convince you of the bias of the Seminar's agenda like reading their own forthright preface in this volume. Beginning-intermediate.

Michael J. Wilkins and J. P. Moreland, *Jesus Under Fire* (Grand Rapids, Mich.: Zondervan, 1995). A collection of scholarly responses to the Jesus Seminar and similar current attacks on the biblical Jesus, the volume includes chapters by Darrell Bock, Gary Habermas, and William Lane Craig. Intermediate.

Philip Yancey, *The Jesus I Never Knew* (Grand Rapids, Mich.: Zondervan, 1995). Popular author Yancey does a remarkable job of shattering preconceived images of Jesus to let the biblical God-man shine through. Beginning-intermediate.

CHAPTER SEVEN

HUMANITY: GOOD NEWS AND BAD NEWS

MOST OF THE TIME, I'M AN OPTIMIST. WHEN I'M PRESENTED with a new situation or meet a new person, I generally expect the best. But I do appreciate the pessimists of the world, so much so that I married one. Of course, Jan insists she's not a pessimist, just a realist. She often has greeted my exuberance over life with something like "Wake up and smell the cat box; it needs changing." It's quite true that I'm the dreamer of the family, and she's the one who sees the practical realities needing attention.

"The optimist proclaims that we live in the best of all possible worlds . . . and the pessimist fears that this is true," said novelist James Branch Cabell. So which way of seeing the world—and of viewing people—is more accurate? Are the optimists right in seeing the world as filled with interesting, good-hearted people to meet and exciting adventures just waiting to be explored? Or are the pessimists correct in assuming that there are dangers and evil people out there waiting to hurt you if you aren't careful?

Will the Real Me Please Stand Up?

Since the beginning of recorded human history, philosophers, theologians, and more recently, psychologists have pondered the question "What is our basic human nature?" Another way of asking the question is "When you strip away all our learned responses, all our societal conditioning, what is the essential inner core common to all people everywhere?" As I have studied this question, I have found the answers falling into one of four categories.

Basically good. A common view in Western culture today is that we are born basically good with a thin veneer of bad. Our inner core is beautiful, but society (or faulty socialization) has laminated our personality with an outer layer of bad. In this view, all that is necessary is for a counselor to help us get through the outer layer and then everything underneath will be pure and beautiful. This is the view of theological liberalism and many secular "humanistic" psychologists, such as Abraham Maslow, Carl Rogers, and others.

Basically neutral. This view is actually a denial that we have any given, underlying nature. It holds that we are born *tabula rasa* (with a "clean slate"). As we grow up, our environment and experiences write on us, and we gradually become good or evil (or more likely, some mixture of each). In other words, we are born basically neutral and made good or bad by conditioning. This is the view of behavioristic psychologists such as John B. Watson, B. F. Skinner, and their many followers in the psychological profession.

Basically evil. A third view is the opposite of the first; we are born basically bad with a thin veneer of good. According to this view, we are born selfish and evil but our parents and society teach us to smile and say "Please" and "Thank you" so we can appear good on the outside. However, underneath there is still the evil, true nature lurking. Many people, including many nonChristians, think this is the biblical view of human nature. Actually, very few Christian theologians have held this view throughout history, and even fewer hold it today. (It has only been the view of some Calvinists and Catholics.)

The biblical view. If the Bible does not teach that we are basically good, neutral, or evil, then what is the scriptural view of basic human nature? The biblical view is actually more complex than any we have considered so far. The Bible says we were originally created totally good, but because of the Fall, we are now born hopelessly fallen. Instead of picturing the human personality like a seedless grape (a thin skin surrounding the "real fruit"), the biblical view is that we are more like an onion. You can keep peeling off layer after layer and never get to the "pure inner core." The biblical view is that each of the layers of our personality was created as good, beautiful, and wholesome by God, but due to the Fall, each layer is now tainted by sin.

Above the fireplace in our living room is a beautiful cherry mantelpiece my wife bought years ago at an estate auction. In the center is a large antique mirror. The glass is now warped and distorted with age, and in several places there are gray spots where the silvering has worn off. Would it surprise you if I say I never take my razor into the living room and use that mirror to shave by? The reflection it casts is no longer perfect. If I shaved by its distorted and incomplete image, I would increase the chances of cutting myself or missing some of my whiskers. So instead I use the newer, but far less elegant, mirror in the bathroom. Its image is still clear and undistorted by the ravages of time.

The biblical picture of our nature is a little bit like our elegant old mirror. The human personality was created by a Master Craftsman to perfectly reflect His image. As a result of the Fall, that image is now cracked, crazed, and distorted beyond any hope of repair in this world. But (as we will see in the next section) His image has not been totally destroyed; the mirror has not been pulverized into dust. We can still see in human nature the beauty of His image, though dim, distorted, and imperfect. Mixed through the layers of our fallen personality, we find beauty placed there by God, as well as the ugly distortion caused by sin. Both are present in the human personality all the way down to the core of who we are.

What is our basic human nature as we are now born into this world? In short, we are wonderfully made and hopelessly fallen. The optimist and the pessimist are both partly right when it comes to human nature.

It's the Image That Counts

When I received Christ as a sophomore in college, I began a long process of reevaluating my pre-Christian lifestyle, attitudes, and interests. As a teenager, I had developed a strong attraction to the arts: music, literature, visual art, and drama. But now some of my new Christian friends warned me, "You must stop listening to and looking at things created by nonChristians. Those people are fallen and their art is worthless. What they create is inspired by the Devil and will lead you away from God. You must give attention only to things made by Christians; only Christian art has any value."

I sincerely wanted to please God and grow in Christ. So I pondered, *Must I really give up experiencing any works of art unless they were produced by Christians?* Was everything else worthless? What confused me was that so much of what Christians were producing (especially in America) seemed so shallow and mediocre. Were my values really so skewed that I couldn't recognize quality when I saw (or heard) it? As I looked at history, some great music, art, and literature was produced by Christians who lived godly lives. But for every Bach, Rembrandt, and Donne there was a Mozart, a Gauguin, and a Flaubert. Why did I find it so hard to dismiss everything produced by nonChristians as worthless? I found the solution to my dilemma in the very beginning of the Bible.

The first chapter of Genesis declares that God made the human race in His image. But what exactly does this mean? Another way of asking the question is: What sets us apart from the rest of the creatures God made on this earth? Through the centuries, theologians, anthropologists, and psychologists have tried to establish what makes us different from animals. Their proposals fall into two broad categories. In the first category are suggestions that the image of God is some ability or capacity that God has given us. Such a view is often called a "constitutional" understanding of God's image in humanity. Some think it is our ability to use reason that makes us unique. Others suggest it is self-awareness or morality or spirituality. People have been making such identifications of the image of God for centuries.

More recently, some theologians have suggested that the image does not have to do with some ability or aspect of the way God has constituted us as individuals. Rather, they suggest the "image" is found in our God-given responsibility or relatedness. Both of these nonconstitutional views are argued from the context in which the Bible first mentions that we are made in God's image. After Genesis declares that "God created man in His own image," the verse goes on to elaborate, "male and female He created them."[1] Theologians like Karl Barth understand this to mean that just as God has eternally been in relationship among the members of the Trinity, so God made us in relationship between men and women. Other theologians cite the next verse in which God commands Adam and Eve to "rule . . . over every living thing that moves on the earth." These scholars assert that it is this role of rulership that makes us different.

My own view is that perhaps all of these mentioned are a part of the image—of what makes us unique from the rest of God's earthly creation. Even if the Bible is not explicit about what the image is, it is clear that all human beings, even nonChristians, still retain the image of God.

"Wait a minute," some might object. "Didn't Adam (and the whole human race) lose the image in the Fall? Maybe it's only when you become a Christian that you regain the image." The problem with this view is the way the idea of the image is used in the rest of the Bible. In Genesis 9, after the Fall and after the great Flood, we see how God made a covenant with Noah. As a part of this covenant, He prohibited murder, saying, "Whoever sheds man's blood, by man his blood shall be shed" (verse 6). God went on to explain why: "For in the image of God He made man." God did not tell Noah, "Don't murder people who believe in Me because they've been given back My image, but go ahead and slaughter as many nonbelievers as you like!" (The New Testament also prohibits verbal abuse of "men, who have been made in the likeness of God," James 3:9.)

This idea that all humans, no matter how evil their behavior, still retain a significant remnant of the image of God was the linchpin for the answer to my question concerning nonChristian art. Because nonbelievers still retain much of God's image, they can still perceive the truth and produce music, art, and literature that reflect beauty and convey transcendence. (As we will see later in this chapter, because of the Fall, it is also true that no artist is entirely free from sin, falsehood, or ugliness.) I began to understand that as a Christian I needed to carefully and prayerfully weigh the value, in terms of intent and message and aesthetic beauty, of all art, whether by Christians or nonChristians. Both can be ugly or beautiful. Both can reflect what is true or what is false.

There is a second and, in our own time, more urgent reason why we need to see all humans as made in the image of God. That is because we live in a time when human life is held increasingly cheap. The value of human beings is being challenged at both ends of life. Since 1973 it has been legal in the United States to abort an unborn human baby at virtually any point in the pregnancy. And there is increasing pressure to liberalize laws regarding "mercy killing." This makes sense if we are nothing more than animals with big brains. However, if the Bible is right and all humans, from the moment of conception until the final flicker of life, are uniquely endowed with the very image of the eternal God, then human life—all human life—is to be treasured and honored and protected.[2]

We Are His Handiwork

Many school systems and courts have battled the question of creation versus evolution during the past seventy-five years since the famous Scopes "monkey trial." However, in my opinion, the media (and so most Americans) have missed an important point in the controversy. The real battle is not (or at least should not be) between evolution and creation, nor between biblical fundamentalists and scientists. The media normally present only two options. But in fact, there are at least four distinct positions. I'll briefly define the four viewpoints and then discuss what I believe is the crucial issue missing in much of the current public debate.

Atheistic evolution. This view says that life on this earth developed gradually over millions of years, and it all happened through the natural mechanism of blind chance working through mutation and natural selection. There is no God or external intelligent force guiding the process.

Theistic evolution. Those who hold this view agree that life developed gradually over millions of years. They, however, see God behind the natural mechanisms guiding and directing the process.

Progressive creationism. This viewpoint agrees that the earth is millions of years old, and the first life appeared early in the earth's history. However, God intervened in the natural processes many times with acts of special creation to bring forth the various species, including humanity.

Special (six-day) creationism. Special creationists view the earth as young (about ten thousand years old) and understand the early chapters of Genesis to teach that God created the earth, all the plants and animals, and the first humans in six, literal twenty-four-hour days.

In most media coverage only the first and last positions are presented. And it's done in caricature fashion: all serious scientists are atheists and all those who believe the Bible are six-day creationists. But many Christian scholars (perhaps the majority) hold one of the middle two views. This simplistic reporting has, in my view, obscured that critical point. The major difference between believers and nonbelievers is not whether they believe in evolution or even whether they view the earth as millions of years old. The primary difference between believers and nonbelievers is whether we humans owe our existence to blind chance or to God. If God is our Creator, no matter how He did it, then we are morally and spiritually accountable to Him. If we are the products of blind chance, then we are accountable to no one but ourselves or (perhaps) each other. Whichever of the last three views a Christian holds, one truth is clear: we are not cosmic accidents; we are valuable creatures of the divine Designer.[3]

So this is the "good news" about human nature. We all (even nonChristians) are made by God in His image and are therefore valuable, beautiful, worthy of protection, and capable of making significant contributions to human culture. But that, of course, is not the whole story.

Murphy Theology

"Anything that *can* go wrong, *will* go wrong," states Murphy's Law. When we think about this, we tend to laugh and grimace at the same time. It is so true to our human experience. It seems whenever we set out to do anything, there is some unseen gremlin running along just ahead of us, tossing obstacles in our path. Why is it that reality seems to so universally resist our best efforts?

The answer is found in the early chapters of the Bible. After God's creative work reached its epitome in the creation of the human race, God looked at all He had made and saw that "it was very good."[4] But this condition of universal perfection did not last long. When the first human parents ate the banned fruit, the results of their rebellion spread like ripples in a pond. First, they became self-conscious and ashamed and covered their bodies.[5] Next, they feared God and hid from

Him.[6] Then, the woman fell out of her natural relation to her own body, resulting in pain in childbirth.[7] Finally, the ground itself began to resist human efforts at cultivation. Originally Adam was to work in joyous cooperation with the earth (Genesis 2:5 uses a Hebrew word that means to "serve" or "dress"). But now, one of the consequences of the Fall is that humans must fight with the earth to gain their food. Although the passage doesn't directly say so, it seems that all human work, not just gardening and farming, is now accomplished only with sweat and frustration.[8]

Because of the Fall, we are now born in a state of being out of proper relation to ourselves, our bodies, other people, and even our environment. Human life, which God intended to be an experience of fulfilling cooperation, has become instead an endless battle of toil, difficulty, and often defeat. Frustration with our own bodies, with other people, with our environment, and with the course of life in general can easily lead to cynicism and even hopelessness.[9] This explosion of trouble didn't end with Adam and Eve; the ripple set in motion by their sin expanded to encompass the entire human race.[10] None of us fulfills the glorious potential God intended in His original creation of the human race. "All have sinned and fall short of the glory of God."[11]

All of this came through to me quite clearly during my first visit to Russia in 1991, shortly before the breakup of the Soviet Union. One of my initial tasks was to engage a Russian-English interpreter to work with me each day for the first week. I found a highly skilled student named Sasha at a linguistics institute in Moscow. I told him that I would need his services every day for the next week and asked him to clear his schedule. We agreed on a price and shook hands on the deal.

After Sasha left for the day, our American director informed me that one of Sasha's professors at the institute had already been hired as my interpreter and paid for the entire week in advance. I dreaded breaking the news to Sasha the next morning. When he arrived and I told him what had happened, I was surprised that he did not seem upset. As I began to apologize profusely for the third time, Sasha held up his hand to silence me.

"You do not need to say any more," he said, his young face impassive. "I understand. I grew up here."

Suddenly I caught a glimpse of what it must have been like for Sasha and his parents who had grown up in this communist society. For all of them, life had been a string of broken promises and unfulfilled expectations. Sasha knew instinctively what we in the West often overlook. Human life and all human enterprise is plagued by obstacle and disappointment. Murphy's Law is always operative because we are all children of the Fall.

Good News and Bad

So, who is right—the optimist or the pessimist? I think the biblical answer is that both the optimist and the pessimist are seeing an aspect of truth about the world and human nature. There is much in the human race that is admirable and praiseworthy. But a thoughtful look at human society and history leaves us with the uneasy feeling that we are much less than we could have been—as individuals and as a race.

That is precisely how God sees us. We humans have been created in God's image and endowed with wonderful talents and potential. But human lives, as lived in this fallen world, at their best fall hopelessly short of what God meant for them to be. At their worst they are endless misery. A study of biblical anthropology (what God has told us about human nature) contains both good news and bad news. The good news is that God has made us humans wonderful, talented, and beautiful; we're the pinnacle of His earthly creation. The bad news is that we have all fallen far short of what God intended us to be.

Now that we have taken a brief look at how God sees the fallen human race, we are ready for some truly good news. In the next chapter we'll explore God's solution to our biggest problem.

■ FOR PERSONAL REFLECTION ■

1. Do you tend to be an optimist or a pessimist? How does this affect your view of yourself? How does it affect your view of God and how you see His view of you?
2. Which of the four views of human nature (basically good, basically neutral, and so forth) do most of the people around you hold? Which view did you hold before reading this chapter? Has the chapter changed your view? If so, how?
3. How should seeing all humans as made in the image of God affect your view of yourself? How should it affect your view of others?
4. In what ways has the Fall affected your own life? How has it affected the lives of the people around you?

■ GROUP DISCUSSION GUIDE ■

1. Pair share: In twos, have each person share whether he or she tends more toward optimism or toward pessimism and then go on to share one incident from the last year or so that illustrates the tendency.
2. What are some ways the message of the Bible is optimistic? What are some ways it is pessimistic?
3. What are some ways that understanding that God's image is in every person affects how we treat other people? What are some ways this doctrine might affect the activities and priorities of the church?
4. What are some ways the effects of the Fall are evident in our society today? In the Christian church in our country? In our own lives as Christians?

■ RECOMMENDED READING ■

Michael J. Behe, *Darwin's Black Box: The Biochemical Challenge to Evolution* (New York: Free Press, 1996). Lehigh

University biochemist Behe argues persuasively that the chemistry of the human cell makes evolution impossible and points instead to intelligent design. Intermediate.

G. C. Berkouwer, *Man: The Image of God* (Grand Rapids, Mich.: Eerdmans, 1962). A thorough examination of the doctrine of the image of God in humanity from an excellent Reformed scholar. Intermediate-advanced.

Philip E. Johnson, *Darwin on Trial* (Downers Grove, Ill.: InterVarsity, 1991). A University of California at Berkeley law professor takes on the scientific establishment. This book has drawn a big reaction from Darwinians. Beginning-intermediate.

Hugh Ross, *Creation and Time* (Colorado Springs, Colo.: NavPress, 1994). Astronomer Ross argues for old-earth (progressive) creationism. Intermediate.

Charles C. Ryrie, *Basic Theology* (Wheaton, Ill.: Victor, 1987). In this concise work, systematic theologian Ryrie gives good though brief coverage of the doctrine of humanity. He argues for a literal, six-day creation. Intermediate.

CHAPTER EIGHT

SALVATION: GOD'S ANSWER TO OUR NEED

IN 1976 THE SLOGAN "I FOUND IT!" SUDDENLY APPEARED ON television, radio, billboards, and bumper stickers everywhere in the United States. The enigmatic phrase was the centerpiece of the first phase of a national evangelistic campaign led by Campus Crusade for Christ. Eventually the whole phrase was revealed: "I found it, new life in Jesus Christ." In the months following the campaign, several other bumper stickers appeared, parodies of the original slogan. One of the most intriguing featured the star of David and the phrase "We never lost it!"

This is a sentiment surprisingly reminiscent of the situation facing the first-century church. The Jewish people in the time of Christ believed they merited salvation simply because they were descendants of Abraham. In a similar fashion, many people today aren't interested in salvation because they don't understand what they need to be saved from. In other words, they don't desire salvation because they don't know they are lost! And yet the evidence that we in the West are lost is all around us. A majority of marriages end in divorce. Most people don't have a close, loving relationship with both their biological parents. Citizens don't consider their leaders trustworthy. Many young people assume they will be less successful than their parents.

Our challenge as Christians is to show how the salvation Christ won at the cross holds the answer to the particular forms of human lostness appearing at the beginning of the twenty-first century. We must proclaim how Christ's death can save our marriages, our families, our governments, and our futures. We need to reveal that we, as individuals and as a culture, have "lost it." We need to explain how all that we've lost can be found in Christ's salvation.

GOD CHOSE US BEFORE WE CHOSE HIM

I want to begin our look at salvation with the teaching I consider to be the most confusing, controversial, and complex of all the subjects in this book: the doctrine of election. You may be thinking, *He just said we need to show the practical relevance of salvation; now he's talking about election. How abstract and irrelevant can you get!* But please bear with me. I believe that election is a crucial and very practical doctrine. Let's begin by defining what we mean.

Election is simply God's choice to save certain individuals.[1] Closely related to election is predestination. This simply means that a destination has been chosen or determined in advance. In the case of salvation, predestination means that our final destination (heaven or hell) was determined, or "destined," in advance.

Part of the reason we in the West have so much trouble with this idea is the tremendous emphasis and value we place on the concept of freedom in our personal and public lives. We like to view ourselves as free in everything, as the "captains of our fate." However, in many areas of our lives we have no choice at all. As Charles Ryrie correctly observes, "We were born into different families; our IQs are not the same; we are of different races; we have varied opportunities in life, etc."[2] Depending on our viewpoint, we see such things as determined by chance, fate, human choice, or God.

But what about our salvation? Is that something determined solely by God, or does our free choice play a role in determining whether we are saved or damned? Christian thinkers have not agreed on the solution to this problem. Throughout the history of Christian thought there have essentially been three answers to the question of who determines our salvation. The three most common answers are (1) God is the primary chooser; (2) we are the primary choosers; and (3) both God and humans choose without creating a contradiction.

Is God the One Who Chooses?

Many Calvinists give the answer that ultimately God chooses who will be saved, and our human choice plays no part at all in this decision.[3] Calvinists cite verses such as Romans 9:15, which quotes God in the Old Testament as saying, "I WILL HAVE MERCY ON WHOM I HAVE MERCY, AND I WILL HAVE COMPASSION ON WHOM I HAVE COMPASSION." Verse 16 adds that it "*does* not *depend* on the man who wills or the man who runs, but on God who has mercy."

Calvinists maintain that God alone determines who comes to Him. They think it only *appears* to us that we have free choice in salvation. For them, our choice was determined (predestined) in advance (see Acts 4:28). Before time began, God chose who would accept and follow Christ (see Ephesians 1:5, 11). Then He draws those same individuals until they do, in fact, come to Him (see John 6:37). Calvinists believe that God is the sole chooser of those who are saved, and human choice plays no part at all. Before the foundation of the world, God chose the elect, and our choosing to come to Christ later in time is the result of God's choice and no part of the cause of our salvation.

Am I the One Who Chooses?

Other Christian thinkers of a more Arminian or Wesleyan bent insist that God's choice is based on what He knows we will choose.[4] In this view, we make the ultimate decision whether to accept the free gift of salvation, and God simply honors our choice (although He does so before we actually choose). Because God can see the future, He knows in advance who will freely come to Christ and He "predestines" them (see Romans 8:28-29).

In this view, I am the one who has the final say in whether I come to Christ or not. God is merely responding in advance to what I will freely choose. Those with Arminian leanings cite the invitation of Revelation 22:17: "Let the one who wishes take the water of life without cost."[5] They argue that any individual can be saved. It is a gift freely offered to all. So if some are elected by God before the foundation of the world, it must be based on the free choice that God knows they are going to make.

Do Both God and I Choose?

Still other Christians believe that both God and humans choose. However, the exact way these choices interact is a mystery, largely beyond human understanding (see 1 Corinthians 2:7). I see in Scripture a clear teaching that God elects and predestines who will be saved.[6] I also see evidence that God holds all humans responsible to do good, not evil, even after the Fall.[7] In addition, God repeatedly urged sinners to repent, turn to Him, and believe.[8] It doesn't make sense that God would continually urge us to believe, if our choice has nothing to do with whether we end up as believers or nonbelievers. Somehow it must be true both that God has the final say in who will be saved and also that our free choice plays a crucial role. One way to think of this might be to say that God is in overall control of history and each person's life, but He has left pockets of free choice within His sovereignty.[9]

The difficulty we have with accepting that both could be true is that, in our own experience of human society, there normally

can be only one person who has the final say. In any human organization, whether business, government, or the church, to the
extent one group has sovereignty, the sovereignty of others is
compromised or limited. While this observation may be true of
all human organizations, it does not follow that God is necessarily unable to make it possible for both of us to choose without
conflict or contradiction.

Recently I presented some of these ideas in a church Sunday
school class. A young woman came up excitedly afterward.
"I've solved the problem," she said with a big smile on her face.
"I know how both we and God can have the final say without
it being a contradiction!"

"I can't wait to hear it," I said with interest. I was glad to
see her wrestling with this ancient question.

"It's like the light in my hallway at home," she said. "The
switches at both ends of the hallway have to say 'On' or the light
is off. So God and each person both have a switch or a free will.
Both have to say yes for the person to be saved."

"I have only one question," I said. "Does God say no to
anyone?"

"No," she said. "Because of Christ's death, God has said yes
to everyone!"

"That's a valid position and an interesting and clear analogy with which to explain it," I told her. "I'm glad to see you
thinking it through."

What I did not have the heart to tell her was that her position was classic Arminianism. Arminians believe that Christ died
for all and that all may therefore come to Him just by saying yes
by faith. She was simply reinventing the view that says that we
have the final say.[10]

The story of my Sunday school student illustrates how difficult it is for us to get our finite minds around the idea that the
final decision could genuinely be both ours and God's.

C. S. Lewis understood how difficult it was to conceive but
he himself held the view that predestination and free choice were

both true. In an appendix to his classic work *Miracles,* Lewis attempted to build up a series of increasingly more nuanced analogies to illustrate this view. He ended with the picture of two dancers (God and each of us) who seamlessly adapt their steps to each other's free choices.[11]

Lewis's analogy reminds me of a story I once heard of a beginning dancer who had the opportunity to take a spin around the ballroom with the legendary Fred Astaire. She later reported, "He was so gentle and subtle as he adjusted to my every falter and misstep, I almost believed I was the expert!" I believe God is artful enough to take even our inept free choices and weave them into an intricate pattern that fits His grand design.[12]

For many centuries there have been, and there still are today, sincere, biblically sound Christians who hold all three views of how election and free will fit together. And I believe that a person can hold any of the three views (or even be ignorant of the debate) and still be a genuine Christian. Therefore, I would consider this a persuasion-level issue.[13]

CHRIST DIED FOR US

When we read the Bible, we sometimes come across words that are difficult to understand, that sound like technical theological jargon. Few people use "propitiation" or "redemption" in everyday conversation.[14] Not only do words like these make the Bible harder to understand; they also can give the false impression that God the Holy Spirit didn't really want to communicate with any but the most religious or highly educated. The truth is that these complex words often conveyed simple, powerful word pictures to their original Greek-speaking readers. Their impact, and perhaps even their clarity, has been lost by translation into the English language. So, let's look at several of these word pictures and see if we can reinvest these less familiar English words with some of the power they held in first-century Greek.

God's Wrath Turned (Propitiation)

The biblical teaching that Christ's death on the cross turned away God's anger against sin brings together several of the doctrines we have already studied in this book. In chapter 3 we learned that God is righteous. In chapter 7 we learned that the Fall caused us to lose our intimate fellowship with God. The biblical word "propitiation" teaches us that Christ's sacrifice on the cross turned away, or satisfied, God's righteous wrath against sin. In Hebrews we are told that Jesus became a High Priest "to make propitiation for the sins of the people."[15] This term would have created a powerful word picture, particularly for the Jewish Christians to whom Hebrews was addressed.

The Greek word for propitiation, *hilasterion*, is translated "mercy seat" in Hebrews 9:5. For the Jewish believers, *hilasterion* would call up the vivid image of the Day of Atonement when the high priest entered the Holy of Holies and poured the blood of a defect-free lamb on the golden cover of the ark of the covenant. This golden surface where the blood spilled was called the mercy seat. At the end of this ritual, the children of Israel knew that their sins were covered for another year and God's righteous wrath toward them would be turned away. In using this same word for what Christ did on the cross, God was painting a vivid word picture of Jesus, the perfect Lamb of God, whose shed blood satisfies God's wrath against our sin.

Sin's Slaves Freed (Redemption)

There was nothing more common in the first century than slavery. Every city in the Roman world had a slave market where conquered foreign citizens were sold to wealthy, local residents. New Testament writers such as Luke, Paul, and John borrowed the words and images of this dreadful custom to make vivid what God has done for us.

"Redemption" was the term used for buying a slave out of the slave market. One of several Greek words translated "redemption" or "redeemed," *exagorazo* pictures a slave being purchased from the market and freed. The Greeks and Romans customarily put a mark on the freed slave's wrist or forehead so that he or she could never be sold into slavery again. This is a beautiful picture of Christ buying us out of slavery and putting the mark of His Holy Spirit on us so we need never again be slaves of Satan or sin.

Christ Trades Places (Substitutionary Death)

The New Testament not only says Christ died for our sins; it actually states that on the cross Jesus *became* sin. Speaking of what the Father did to the Son on the cross, Paul said, "He made Him who knew no sin to be sin on our behalf."[16] It seems impossible to imagine how Jesus could become so completely identified with our sin that it could say that He was made to "be sin." If this was not in the Bible, I would not dare to say it—it seems almost blasphemous. But what a wonderful trade this is for us! He gets the penalty for our sin; we get the free gift of His right-standing before God. He gets what He did not deserve; we get what we could not possibly earn.

Fellowship Restored (Reconciliation)

The result of Christ's work on the cross (which includes propitiation, redemption, and substitution) is that we fallen, estranged humans can be reconciled, brought back into fellowship with God. This reconciliation has two parts. On the cross Christ's sacrifice *reconciled God to us.* Paul told the Corinthian believers that God "reconciled us to Himself through Christ, and . . . that God was in Christ reconciling the world to Himself, not counting their trespasses against them."[17] However, reconciliation isn't complete until *we become reconciled to God.* Again, Paul told the Corinthians that God "has committed to us the word of reconciliation. Therefore, we are ambassadors for Christ, as though God were entreating through us; we beg you on behalf of Christ, be reconciled to God."[18]

This is the reason that all are not saved just because Christ died on the cross. Yes, God was reconciled to us: His righteous anger was satisfied, the price for our freedom was paid, and Christ took the penalty of death in our place. However, all of these things did not achieve a full restoration of fellowship between us and God. One thing remains: we sinners, who are God's enemies, must turn and embrace Him, accepting the gift of Christ's death and the new life He freely offers. Then the reconciliation is complete.

As with the issue of election, my particular understanding of these biblical words is a persuasion, not a conviction. What all true Christians hold in common, and what I think should be defended at a conviction level of belief, is the teaching that Christ's death on the cross is what made it possible for us to have a restored relationship with God.

WE RECEIVE HIM BY FAITH

One of the great cries of the Reformation was *sola fides,* which means "only by faith." The Roman Catholic Church at that time was teaching that doing good works and receiving the sacraments were necessary in addition to faith. Luther, Calvin, and the other early Protestants rediscovered the biblical teaching that "by grace you have been saved through faith."[19] They began to preach again that salvation is "not as a result of works, that no one should boast."[20] God does His part, which is grace (reconciling Himself to us through Christ's death). To be saved, we must do our part, which is faith (responding to His initiative and being reconciled to Him).

Although historic Protestants in general, and contemporary evangelicals in particular, agree that all that is necessary for salvation on the part of humans is faith, they have not always agreed on the exact nature of faith. Since the late 1980s, much disagreement over the nature of faith has centered on the issue of "lordship salvation."

The Lordship Salvation Controversy

Put in very simple terms, some evangelicals think faith means simply believing that Christ is God and accepting the free gift of forgiveness He offers. Others say that a personal, whole-life commitment of "accepting Christ as Lord" is necessary for salvation. This controversy, which has always been a minor theme within American evangelicalism, moved to the status of a central issue with the 1988 publication by John MacArthur, Jr., of *The Gospel According to Jesus*. Let's look more closely at the two sides of the issue and then consider a mediating view.

Merely rational assent? Some contemporary Christian theologians, such as Charles Ryrie and Zane Hodges, believe that faith means merely giving mental assent that certain things are true. For them, saving faith is simply believing that Jesus is God, who died for our sins, and can forgive us and give us eternal life.[21] Although these writers would say that we should repent of our sins and have a change of life, these are not prerequisites for salvation.[22]

Passionate commitment? Other current Christian writers stress that saving faith must include a passionate abandonment of the whole person—a lordship decision.[23] These Christians view repentance as a necessary part of faith.[24] For them, a true gospel message must include a call for a radical change of heart and will, a "spiritual crisis."[25]

Faith as trust (a middle view). Biblical faith is nothing more (and nothing less) than trust. In fact, the same root word in Greek is translated by both English words *faith* and *believe*. The biblical view of saving faith seems to be more than Ryrie defines it to be but perhaps something less than MacArthur would like. Saving faith does involve a commitment of the will to give our whole selves over to Christ. So, true biblical faith is more than simply mental assent to certain doctrinal propositions.

Someone has said, "Coming to Christ is giving all of myself that I know to all of God that I know."[26] This is a good way to think of it. As a nineteen-year-old, I did not know much about God or much about my own sinful heart. But when I received

Christ, I turned over all that I knew of myself to God as I then understood Him. As I have walked with Christ, I have discovered many areas I was not initially aware of, and I have needed to turn those over to His loving control.

Saving faith involves a commitment of all that I have to give to all that I know of Christ. This focuses on the attitude involved in faith, rather than on specific behavior changes. Suppose a young woman comes to Christ. What if she knows little of how her life displeases God, or if she has little control of herself through addiction or other emotional impairments? Then a full commitment would involve giving only a small portion of herself (but still all she possesses). Likewise, if her knowledge of Christ is minimal or faulty (a common condition for one just becoming a Christian), then she can only give herself to the Christ she knows. Paul says that saving faith "is the gift of God."[27] Her part in faith is to take the opportunity now restored to her and respond with all she possesses (however much or little that might be).

The biblical idea of repentance is contained within faith. When I turn from whatever I was trusting before (myself, good luck, another religion) and begin trusting my life to Christ, that is true repentance. It may or may not involve turning from specific, sinful behavior, depending on what I know of God's righteousness and what I know of my own sinfulness.

What I believe should be held at the conviction level is that we are saved by faith, not as a result of our own good works. The lordship-salvation controversy has been a discussion among true believers over the exact nature of that saving faith. Both Ryrie and MacArthur would, I am confident, acknowledge that the other is a true believer, a brother in Christ. So I would class the whole lordship discussion as a persuasion-level disagreement.

Some Truly Good News
The message of salvation is good news because it fulfills people's deepest desires. It meets the special needs and longings of those living in our current Western culture and in every other culture.

The gospel makes sense of why the world is such a mess and why our every attempt to improve it seems to generate yet another problem. It offers a genuine value to each of our lives that is not dependent on wealth, physical beauty, position, or power. It provides a way to begin to heal our inner hurts, our broken relationships, and our unjust societal structures. It provides a realistic hope for the future of the world and for eternal life.

■FOR PERSONAL REFLECTION■

1. Who do you think has the final say in our salvation: God or us? How would you argue for your answer with someone who disagreed?

2. Which of the four biblical word pictures is now most vivid and meaningful to you (propitiation, redemption, substitutionary death, or reconciliation)?

3. Where do you stand in the lordship-salvation controversy? Do you think your position on this issue makes any practical difference in your Christian life (or how you share Him with others)? Why or why not?

■GROUP DISCUSSION GUIDE■

1. Brainstorm: Have the group think of as many reasons as they can why so many in our country are not interested in (or do not think they need) salvation. (Do not evaluate; just have someone write the reasons on a board or on a piece of paper.)

2. What practical value does the doctrine of election (God chose us) have for our Christian lives?

3. Which of the four word pictures (propitiation, redemption, substitutionary death, and reconciliation) is most emotionally gripping for you and why?

4. Do you think faith is primarily rational assent or passionate commitment, or is it both? Explain your answer.

5. What would be some practical ways we might show the
importance of salvation to those who are apathetic about
their need?

■ RECOMMENDED READING ■

Paul Enns, *The Moody Handbook of Theology* (Chicago: Moody,
1989). Enns gives an excellent overview of the entire doctrine of salvation in a brief chapter 24. Intermediate.

Zane C. Hodges, *Absolutely Free!* (Dallas, Tex.: Redencion
Viva, 1989). A popular-level response to MacArthur by a
former Dallas Seminary professor who argues that faith is
merely rational assent. Beginning-intermediate.

**C. S. Lewis, "Appendix B: On 'Special Providences'" in
*Miracles, A Preliminary Study*** (New York: Macmillan,
1947), 180-187. In this brief essay, Lewis does the best job
I have seen of envisioning how sovereignty and free will
might both be true. Beginning-intermediate.

John MacArthur, Jr., *The Gospel According to Jesus* (Grand
Rapids, Mich.: Zondervan/Academie, 1988). Pastor and
popular author MacArthur argues persuasively for the lordship-salvation position. Intermediate.

CHAPTER NINE

THE HOLY SPIRIT: OUR INDWELLING COMFORTER

"GOD IS ALREADY USING YOU IN A WONDERFUL WAY, ALAN." The minister peered at me with an intensity that both frightened and fascinated me. "Imagine how much more He could use you if you had the power that comes with the baptism of the Holy Spirit!"

I was a sophomore in college and had received Christ just a few months before. We were on a weekend retreat where the speaker was a former gang leader who had been led to Christ by a Pentecostal minister. Now they both stood over me in their cabin, laid their hands on me, and began to speak in tongues.

"Let the power of the Holy Spirit flow through you," the minister exhorted. "Just let your tongue go free—say the first thing that comes into your head."

I wanted this experience so badly. I still had doubts about my new Christianity. If I could have a real supernatural experience, I thought, then I would know it was true. To possess God's power in a special way—that would make me special.

Fearfully I closed my eyes and opened my mouth, wondering what would come out.

The Long-Neglected Doctrine

Not until the twentieth century has the doctrine of the Holy Spirit been explored in detail. Controversy often spurs the church to formulate a specific doctrine more clearly, and until the early 1900s, the only churchwide controversy involving the Holy Spirit centered on the Spirit's role in the Trinity. Later, with the advent of the modern Pentecostal and charismatic movements, the church as a whole began to debate the role of the Spirit in salvation and in the Christian life.[1]

It is rather surprising, then, to discover that the Bible has quite a bit to say about the third person of the Trinity. In this chapter, we will look briefly at the personality and deity of the Spirit, His activity in various eras of biblical history, and His crucial roles in salvation and in the Christian life. And we'll make an important discovery: To know and enjoy God means, in large part, getting to know and enjoy our relationship with the Holy Spirit.

The Spirit and His Ministry

The Holy Spirit is not an "it" or some kind of force. The Spirit is a Person. By this I mean the Bible reveals that the Spirit possesses all the qualities we usually associate with personhood. The Spirit has a mind.[2] He can be grieved, and so He has emotions.[3] Additionally, He possesses a will, or the ability to choose.[4]

The Bible also clearly teaches that the Spirit is God. He has the attributes of omnipresence,[5] omniscience,[6] and eternality.[7] He participated in the creation of the world[8] and was the agent of the miraculous conception of Christ.[9]

I mentioned in chapter 1 that I hold the doctrine of the Trinity to be a conviction-level belief. If the Holy Spirit is a full and equal member of the Trinity, He must be both personal and divine. These crucial historic teachings of Christianity are also, I believe, conviction-level doctrines.

Throughout the various ages of biblical history, the Holy Spirit has played different roles. While some of the ministries of the Spirit have remained constant over time, there is at least one major difference in His relationship to believers before and since the day of Pentecost.[10]

In the Old Testament. In the chapter on the Bible, I discussed how the Spirit worked in partnership with the human authors of Scripture. In addition, God sent His words to us by the Spirit through the prophets.[11] When the prophets pronounced the will of God, they were said to have God's Spirit "upon them."[12] Even before prophets' words were written down in the Bible, they were a verbal revelation by God to His people through the Holy Spirit.[13]

In relation to believers. The clearest statement in the Bible explaining the difference between the Spirit's relation to believers in the two Testaments came from the mouth of Jesus. He told His disciples, "[The Spirit] abides with you, and will be in you."[14] For pre-Pentecost believers, the Spirit worked primarily as an external influence, indwelling and filling them only temporarily and for special purposes. He filled the artisans who constructed the tabernacle.[15] He filled certain Old Testament leaders—such as Joshua—with wisdom,[16] and He filled others—like the prophet Micah—with power.[17]

In the earthly life of Christ. The Holy Spirit worked in several special ways during Christ's sojourn here on this planet. He anointed Christ to preach.[18] He filled Him[19] and was the source of our Lord's power to cast out demons and perform other miracles.[20] Romans 1:4 seems to teach that the Spirit was even involved in the resurrection of Christ.

In our salvation. The Holy Spirit plays several decisive roles in the salvation of post-Pentecost saints. These roles cover the entire process of salvation, from initial convicting of sin to sealing us for the day of redemption.

- **He convicts us of sin.** Jesus said of the Holy Spirit, "He, when He comes, will convict the world concerning sin, and righteousness, and judgment."[21] The Holy Spirit comes to us before we accept Christ and causes us to believe that we have a need for forgiveness (sin), that there are moral absolutes (righteousness), and that we will be accountable for our failure to live up to those absolute standards (judgment). This ministry of the Spirit to nonbelievers does not guarantee each person will accept these things as true, but only that they will be exposed to these aspects of God's truth.[22] The Holy Spirit often accomplishes these ministries of conviction through the words of the Bible (read or preached) and through the personal witness of believers.

- **He gives us a new birth.** As we learn in John 3, Jesus told Nicodemus that to enter the kingdom of God, a person must be "born again." Nicodemus was confused by this. Similarly, many today do not understand the real meaning of the phrase. The second birth is a supernatural awakening to God of the human spirit that is brought about by the Holy Spirit at the moment of salvation. It is called the "washing of regeneration"[23] because it washes away the guilt of sin and makes us new creatures in Christ.[24] This happens at the moment of saving faith, and it is the new birth that makes us Christians.[25]

- **He indwells us.** Since Pentecost, every true believer is permanently indwelt by the Holy Spirit.[26] This is a change from the status of pre-Pentecost believers. In the Old Testament, as I already mentioned, the Spirit was given temporarily for special service. Even when the Holy Spirit was inside an Old Testament believer, He might be taken away due to disobedience.[27] However, since Pentecost, this is all changed. By the time Paul was writing his letters to the churches, the residence of the Holy Spirit in believers had become certain and secure. In the case of the carnal believers at Corinth,[28] some of whom were involved with pagan temple prostitutes,[29] Paul said that the Holy Spirit was still in them.[30] The indwelling of New Testament believers is permanent.

- **He baptizes us.** The root meaning of the Greek word translated "baptize" is identification. Several sorts of baptism appear in Scripture, and not all of them involve dunking in water. (For example, in the "baptism of Noah," mentioned in 1 Peter 3:20, Noah's family identified themselves with Noah's faith in God. The result was: they all avoided getting wet!) The baptism of the Holy Spirit is the way God identifies us with Himself. It happens at the moment of spiritual birth, not later, as Pentecostals and some charismatics teach.[31]

- **He seals us.** A Roman seal was an assurance that the awesome power of the empire stood behind whatever bore the seal. First-century readers understood that God's seal would have the power of the almighty God behind it. So when Paul wrote of "the Holy Spirit of God, by whom you were sealed for the day of redemption,"[32] the early Christians would have immediately seen this as an absolute, unbreakable promise by God to bring all believers safely to their ultimate salvation.[33]

In our Christian life. In the next chapter, I'm going to talk about the role of the filling of the Spirit in our daily walk as believers. Here I would like to mention briefly several other ministries of the Spirit to each Christian.

- **He teaches us.** Shortly before His crucifixion, Jesus gave His disciples a wonderful promise. He promised that the "Spirit of Truth" would come to guide the disciples' understanding. He promised that the Spirit would help them understand all the things Jesus wanted them to know but which they were not yet mature enough to understand.[34] This teaching ministry of the Spirit works in at least two ways today. First, when we sit down to read our Bible, God's Spirit (the divine Author) is right there with us to help us understand the meaning of what we read.[35] Second, the Holy Spirit works through human teachers.[36] Whenever I stand up to teach, I pray, often aloud with my students, "Father, we ask that You would send Your Holy Spirit to be our Teacher." In my experience, this is a prayer God is always delighted to answer.

- **He leads us.** One of the great privileges of being a Christian is that we can be led and guided by the Holy Spirit.[37] It is often within this arena of subjective, personal leading that God draws us into a more intimate relationship with Himself. We want to know: What should I do with my life? Whom should I marry? What job should I take? How should I spend my money? God uses these uncertainties in our lives to draw us into a close, healthy interdependence with Him.[38] God the Holy Spirit is pleased when we seek His wisdom on any subject, no matter how large or small.[39] The Holy Spirit may answer us through the wise counsel of mature believers, circumstances, or our own godly desires,[40] or even by speaking to us quietly in our minds.[41] However, the Holy Spirit will never lead us to do something that is contrary to the teaching of the Bible. As the divine author of Scripture, the Spirit will not contradict Himself.[42]

Additional ministries of the Spirit to us as believers include helping us to pray,[43] giving us spiritual gifts,[44] and giving us the power to share Christ.[45]

INSTANT SPIRITUAL MATURITY?

As a new Christian, sitting in that cabin with two Pentecostals praying in tongues, I longed for an experience that would bring me instant maturity and drive away all doubt. However, God the

Holy Spirit, in His wisdom, did not allow me to have that experience of speaking in tongues. I think I know why. If I had spoken in tongues that day, in my frame of mind, I would have begun putting my faith in that ecstatic experience, not in God Himself. Instead, He allowed me to learn slowly to walk by faith, to trust Him daily, even when I do not have any special emotional experience.

At various times in my Christian life since then, I have had some wonderful, emotionally powerful experiences with the Lord (although none has ever involved speaking in tongues). But I've learned not to make these experiences the basis of my relationship with God. I have learned to walk with the Lord through rich and fruitful times and through dry and barren times. In the next chapter we will examine in more detail exactly how we grow and walk consistently with the Lord.

■ FOR PERSONAL REFLECTION ■

1. What mental image comes into your mind when you think of the Holy Spirit (a cloud, a ghost, a person, and so on)?
2. What are several things the Holy Spirit did in the Old Testament? How is that different from what He is doing today? How is it the same?
3. How does the Pentecostal view of the baptism of the Holy Spirit differ from the one presented in this chapter? What is your own view, and why?
4. How have you experienced the leading of the Holy Spirit in your own life?

■ GROUP DISCUSSION GUIDE ■

1. Case study: Divide the class or small group into subgroups of three to five individuals. In the subgroups, discuss this case study. "A friend from your work tells you over lunch that he (or she) is a member of the Jehovah's Witnesses. They accept the Bible as true but believe that the Holy

Spirit is just a force of the one God, not a separate person of the Trinity. How could you show him (or her) *from Scripture* that the Holy Spirt is a separate person of the Godhead?" After fifteen minutes, have each group report briefly to the others.

2. Based on what you read in the chapter (or your own knowledge of Scripture), in what ways would our salvation or our Christian lives be affected if there were no Holy Spirit?

3. Is the Holy Spirit currently an important part of your relationship with God? If so, how? If not, why do you think He is not?

4. Have any of you ever spoken in tongues or known someone who has? What part does tongues play in your walk with God? (Or what part do you think God intends tongues to play?)

■ RECOMMENDED READING ■

Michael Green, *I Believe in the Holy Spirit* (Grand Rapids, Mich.: Eerdmans, 1989). British evangelical Green gives a well-reasoned, biblical, and nonPentecostal treatment of all aspects of the Holy Spirit. Intermediate.

J. I. Packer, *Keep in Step with the Spirit* (Old Tappan, N.J.: Revell, 1984). Packer gives a thoughtful and gracious evangelical critique of the charismatic movement. Intermediate.

C. C. Ryrie, *The Holy Spirit* (Chicago: Moody, 1965). In this 120-page book, Ryrie briefly covers the entire doctrine of the Holy Spirit, including an excellent chapter on how to be filled. Beginning-intermediate.

R. C. Sproul, *The Mystery of the Holy Spirit* (Wheaton, Ill.: Tyndale, 1990). Sproul has written a very readable volume from the Reformed perspective that includes excellent chapters on the baptism and fruit of the Spirit. Beginning-intermediate.

CHAPTER TEN

CHRISTIAN GROWTH: OUR WALK OF FAITH

HER NAME WAS JOY, BUT HER FACE WAS ANYTHING BUT joyful. Indeed, it bore the marks of a long inner struggle.

"The Christian life seems hopeless to me." Her shoulders slumped.

"God is so demanding," she continued after a moment. "He's not happy with anything less than absolute perfection!"

"What makes you say that?" I asked.

"Well, there's that verse in First Peter where it says, 'Be ye holy; for I am holy.'[1] I looked it up and Peter was quoting the Old Testament, where God said it repeatedly. That's a pretty tough standard to live up to—the holiness of God."

She let out a long sigh and shook her head. "It reminds me of my parents. Nothing I ever did was good enough to please them. I always fell short."

"What, exactly, do you think it means to be 'holy'?" I asked.

Joy shrugged. "I don't know . . . I guess it means to be morally perfect in everything—to be as righteous as God Himself!"

SET APART FOR A SPECIAL PURPOSE

Joy was struggling with the everyday experience of Christian growth—what theologians call the doctrine of sanctification. The English words *holy* and *sanctify* are both translations of biblical words that have the same root meaning "to be dedicated or set apart." To be holy or sanctified means that we are dedicated and set apart for God's special purpose.

Let me illustrate what I mean. If you are ever a guest in the Scholes's home and we serve your meal on Penrose china, then you will know that we regard you as someone very special indeed. Why? Because we bring out the Penrose china only about once a year. These pieces of china are special and valuable to us for several reasons. First, they have personal value to us because Penrose is my wife's maiden name. Second, they are expensive bone china, manufactured and hand decorated by Minton, one of the oldest English bone china factories in the world, established in 1795. During the last twenty-five years, Jan and I have gradually accumulated the set we now have, mostly as Christmas and birthday presents from Jan's parents. If we broke a piece of the Penrose china, it is unlikely we could afford to replace it. The final reason is that the set is quite valuable. About ten years ago, Minton discontinued the pattern; this china is literally irreplaceable. You can imagine that we do not let little kids take it out to the sandbox for imaginary tea parties!

Our attitude toward the Penrose china is a good example of what the Bible means by the words "holy" and "sanctified." The Penrose china is set apart and dedicated to a rare and special purpose—celebrations with distinguished guests. In the same way, when the Bible talks about "sanctification," it is referring to a process by which we become dedicated and special, set apart by God for His own high and holy purpose.

Joy's confusion about holiness, or sanctification, was at least twofold. First, she thought of holiness as always referring to some form of absolute perfection. Second, she viewed the production of a holy life as her responsibility, something God demanded she do. No wonder she had lost hope! She had a picture of God sitting on His throne like some tyrannical father in the sky, expecting her to perform flawlessly.

Recognizing the Three Phases of Sanctification

The first thing Joy and other defeated, perfectionistic Christians like her need to understand is that, while perfect holiness is God's ultimate goal for every Christian, He does not expect sinless perfection in this life. In fact, the Bible indicates that there are actually three distinct aspects or phases of sanctification, of becoming separated to His holy purpose for us: past, present, and future.

Past. Sometimes when God's Word speaks about sanctification, it is referring to something already true of us from the moment we receive Christ. When Paul wrote to the Corinthians, he bluntly confronted them for being fleshly, contentious, and overtly immoral. But in the same letter, he didn't hesitate to say, "You were sanctified."[2] Theologians call this "positional" or "legal" sanctification. The idea is that we have been given a legal position before God that has nothing to do with our behavior or experience. When we receive Christ as our Savior, many things happen to us. One of them is that we are now "in Christ."[3] When God looks at us, He sees not our sin, our immaturity, or our disobedience. Rather, God the Father sees the perfect holiness of Christ. This position, this place of special privilege, is a result of the gift of salvation, regardless of our behavior.[4]

When I sin, especially when it is my own conscious choice to disobey God, there is a part of me that feels disgusted and disappointed. I feel guilty, ashamed, and small. It is natural for me to imagine God feeling the same way toward me as I do toward myself. At those times it's easy for me to see Him sitting on a huge throne, drumming giant fingers on the ornate armrest, saying, "What's wrong with you, Scholes? Haven't you conquered that sin yet? I thought you'd be much further along by now!"

But the truth is, because of positional sanctification, God can separate His attitude toward *my behavior* from His attitude toward *me*. He hates my sin but He loves me. His acceptance of me is based not on my behavior or progress but on the fact that I am in Christ.

Present. The second aspect of salvation does have to do with our behavior and our experience. Theologians call this "progressive" or "experiential" sanctification. This is the process that goes on from the time we receive Christ until we die. Paul prayed for the Thessalonians, "May the God of peace Himself sanctify you entirely."[5] The sanctification Paul spoke of here was not yet complete, although the Thessalonians were true believers and had therefore already received positional sanctification. This is a progressive aspect of sanctification through which we gradually are made more like Christ in our thoughts, words, and deeds.[6] Because God views us as if we were already completely holy (positional sanctification), His acceptance and approval of us do not have to be based on how close we currently are to His absolute standard of perfection. This gives us the freedom to grow toward perfection without the fear of God's impatient condemnation.[7] We need to understand that, yes, it is God's desire for us to be holy as He is holy. But His desire flows from love, not anger.

Most of our human images of holiness and perfection are badly flawed. It is too easy for us to think of God as like some fussy old spinster aunt who can't stand to have children in her house for fear they will mar her perfectly polished wooden floors or knock over her precious antiques. Our heavenly Father's desire for us to be holy is not because He is offended or impatient with our bumbling immaturity. All of His righteous anger against our sin was poured out on Christ. Rather, it is His love and compassion for us that cause Him to want us to be holy.

Our Father can see clearly the many ways that our lack of sanctification is hurting us. He sees our anxiety and confusion from minds cluttered with the warped and contradictory thoughts of the world. He grieves over the twisted and tormented relationships born from feelings and impulses dominated by the lusts of our flesh. When God looks at our unholy responses, often inadvertent and immature, He does not look with anger but with sadness. Because He loves us more deeply and truly than we love ourselves, He is not satisfied. He wants to free us from the pain we experience as the result of incomplete holiness. He longs for us to know a far better life.

Unfortunately, the word *holy* in our language and thinking has become too closely associated with a "holier-than-thou" attitude. We often envision a "holy" person as aloof, judgmental, and intolerant. God's idea of holiness is almost the opposite. Jesus' earthly life should form our picture of what human holiness or sanctification would look like. He was patient and loving with children. He was kind and compassionate with the weak and broken. His words of condemnation and judgment were reserved for self-righteous religious leaders. With sinners, with the hurt and the poor, Jesus was always gentle and tender.

My youngest daughter, Laura, now a young adult, is a gifted artist whose drawings and paintings have been featured in regional art exhibitions. Of course, she was not always as experienced as she is today. It seems like only a few years ago that she and my other two children would bring home rough crayon scribbles from kindergarten. Would my wife and I, being discerning connoisseurs, say, "What do you mean, bringing these pieces of trash into our beautiful home? You're going to have to do far better than that before you can expect us to display any of your work, even in the garage!"

Of course not! Up they immediately went: on the refrigerator, on the walls, in the bedrooms, in the hallways, until the entire house was filled with the things Laura and our other children had made. We delighted in them because our precious children had offered them to us in joy and pride. Because we praised and encouraged even their earliest and most modest efforts, Laura and the others each grew toward the measure of the artistic gifts they possessed inside.

Can you feel God your heavenly Father smiling at even your hesitant and stumbling efforts at holy living? If you will only bring whatever it is you are and have to Him, He will receive it with joy and give you a big hug. Then He will turn and proudly display for all the angels to see the gift that you, His beloved child, has brought Him.

As I sit at my computer, rereading the last paragraph, I have tears streaming down my face, fogging my glasses. Although I have understood the doctrine of sanctification for many years, it is far too seldom that I feel God's smile. If I could only feel His love for me more often, I have no doubt that I would grow more quickly.

Future. The Bible is clear, however, that none of us (except Jesus) will reach perfect holiness or sanctification in this life.[8] Nevertheless, God in His grace will bring us to a point where we are completely sanctified. Paul wrote to the Colossians that Christ died to present believers to God "holy and blameless and beyond reproach."[9] This will happen at the second coming of Christ, in an instant, at the same moment we receive our immortal bodies.[10] Our sin nature will be removed and then we will be as completely dedicated and set apart in our experience and behavior as we have been positionally, in God's eyes, since the moment we received Christ.[11]

So the first message I would like to give to Joy and others like her is that God is not demanding instant perfection in this life. Rather, because He loves you and already treats you as if you were perfect because of Christ, He invites you to follow Him in a lifelong adventure of continually growing in sanctification.

Becoming Lovable

Joy's second area of confusion was that she saw progress in the Christian life—sanctification—as solely her own responsibility. Instead of an ally who would help her grow, God seemed like a taskmaster who, by His impossible demands, made successful growth hopeless. What Joy did not grasp is that, far from being our enemy in sanctification, God, in the person of the Holy Spirit, is the one who makes sanctification possible.

The liberating truth is that I can no more sanctify myself than I can save myself. Saving faith, as we discussed in chapter 8, is an attitude of trust. It is giving as much of myself as I know to as much of God as I know. When I assume that attitude toward Christ and what He has done on the cross, God the Holy Spirit applies salvation to me by regenerating, indwelling, baptizing, and sealing me. Now, as a Christian, I can grow in holiness *by the same means.*

I used to wonder why God would call David "a man after His own heart."[12] After all, David was a liar, an adulterer, and a murderer! Not at all my idea of a holy man of God. But I think I have gradually begun to understand. God is not primarily interested in our behavior. What He wants most from us is a close, intimate relationship. He longs for us to know Him heart to heart. This was the one thing that distinguished David's life above all else. No matter what he thought, felt, or did, David quickly came back to God and opened his heart. Walking closely with God is not a performance; it is opening one's heart to Him.

Too many Christians, perhaps my friend Joy among them, think Christian growth is somehow harder or is more complex or requires more effort than salvation. However, in Galatians, Paul made it clear that my own good works are of no more use in living the Christian life than they are in obtaining my initial salvation. He asked the Galatian Christians, "This is the only thing I want to find out from you: did you receive the Spirit by the works of the Law, or by hearing with faith? Are you so foolish? Having begun by the Spirit, are you now being perfected by the flesh?"[13] I begin the Christian life by opening my heart to God's Spirit. Sanctification is the lifelong process of learning to open myself continually to the Holy Spirit.

We saw in the last chapter that since Pentecost every true believer has been indwelt by the Holy Spirit from the moment he or she receives Christ. It is the normal state of a Christian to be filled with the Spirit. But just as honeymooning newlyweds eventually have their first quarrel, sooner or later every new believer chooses to disobey God in a conscious act of sin. At that moment the Holy Spirit is grieved and the newfound fellowship with God is broken.[14] In the same way we would reconcile with a human loved one, we restore our broken fellowship with God by coming to Him, admitting our fault, accepting His forgiveness, and opening our hearts to Him once again.[15]

Although there are many similarities between a marriage relationship and our fellowship with God, there are also some crucial differences. When human lovers quarrel, often both partners end up partly at fault. No matter who begins the fight, too often the other becomes angry and says or does things he or she later regrets. So when human lovers reconcile, it often involves one person admitting fault and then the other agreeing that he (or she) was also at fault. However, when we sin against God, although He is grieved, He does not become angry. His anger against sin was dealt with decisively at the cross. All that is necessary to restore fellowship is for us to admit our wrong. God is always ready and anxious to embrace us in fellowship once again, no matter how grievous our sin.

Another difference between a human-human restoration and the divine-human relationship is that human lovers (or friends) often try to restore a relationship without a complete admission of responsibility for their error. A man may say, "Honey, I feel badly about what I said yesterday." She may respond, "Don't worry about it—it was no big deal." They restore their fellowship by trying to minimize and overlook both the offense and the hurt they caused each other. This is a dangerous practice because the offended one(s) may still feel hurt. It can result in the planting of a root of bitterness that later reaches to the surface, causing great trouble.[16] If minimizing or suppressing sin is unwise in strictly human relationships, it is completely useless in our relationship with God. He never minimizes or overlooks our sin. God does, however, forgive it for the sake of Christ whenever we fully confess.[17]

This, then, is the second message I want the Joys of the world to hear. Holiness is not primarily a responsibility, a labor, or an obligation. Christian growth—sanctification—is a relationship. As we continue to open our hearts to our loving Lord through the person of the Holy Spirit living inside of us, the Spirit Himself brings us along on the path toward holiness.

Being filled with the Holy Spirit, then, is becoming lovable. I don't mean that we must clean up our lives to somehow become worthy of God's love. Because of Christ, God the Father, Son, and Holy Spirit stands with arms reaching out toward us. All it takes to become lovable is to relax and accept His loving embrace.

Being filled with the Spirit isn't something strange and unusual, reserved only for a few great spiritual leaders. Rather, being filled was your natural state when you first knew Christ, and it can be your normal, daily experience. Bill Bright, the founder of Campus Crusade, likens the process of being filled to breathing. When we sin through a known act of rebellion or disobedience, we need to breathe spiritually. First, we exhale by confessing (agreeing with God about) our sin. Then, we inhale by trusting that we are again filled and controlled by the Holy Spirit—fellowship with God is restored.[18]

Just as fellowship is the natural state of marriage, and every marriage begins in delight and celebration, so fellowship is the natural state of our relationship with God. We begin our new life with Christ as spiritual beings, filled by the Holy Spirit. Fleshly behavior and disobedience is the unnatural, abnormal state for the Christian. It takes effort to hold ourselves away from fellowship with God, just as it drains our emotional energy to stay mad or upset at a human loved one. Breathing is natural; holding our breath is difficult and uncomfortable.

Enjoying God

The secret of enjoying God is the same as the secret of enjoying a long-term loving relationship with a spouse or close friend. When some rift develops in the relationship, we must become lovable once again. The secret is not to let small rifts in the relationship grow into big ones. Deal with them right away. With other humans this means going to them and talking it out. With God, it means coming to Him, confessing our sin, embracing the joy of His forgiveness, and then moving forward in our relationship, filled with the Spirit.

One aspect of becoming a mature Christian, then, is to "keep short accounts" with God. Whenever we sin, we should agree with Him quickly and continue a close walk of fellowship. There are a number of activities (habits or disciplines) of the Christian life that can help us here. These important habits include Bible study, prayer, and witnessing. Doing these things helps our walk in the Spirit to be more consistent and also gives the Spirit the raw material to develop our character toward that of Christ Himself.

I remember vividly when Jan and I were first married. I was so in love with her! I wanted to spend all of my time with her, gazing at her and talking to her. When she was gone for even a brief period of time, I had to be careful not to bore all my friends by constantly talking about how wonderful a wife I had. If I was alone, I would read and reread the love letters she had written during our months of engagement.

This is a close parallel to how I felt and behaved as a new believer. When I first came to Christ as a college student, I enjoyed times of prayer, both alone and with other believers. Talking with God was not a chore but a privilege and a joy. I wanted to tell all my nonbelieving friends about Christ. Reading the Bible was an adventure of discovery.

As in most marriages, many things eventually hindered the intimacy of my relationship with Jan. Kids, work, illness, bills, family obligations, and travel all conspired to come between us. At first I resisted scheduling appointments to sit down with Jan and just talk. It seemed so regimented, not at all like the wonderfully spontaneous conversations we'd had about everything and nothing when we were first married. But soon I realized that we had to plan time for each other or else we would gradually grow further and further apart.

I've come to the same realization in my relationship with God. While praying, studying the Bible, and sharing my faith came easily as a new believer, now they require discipline or they will get shoved out completely in the busyness of my life. If I am to be lovable, if I am to grow closer in my walk with my Lord, I need to make myself available.

So my message to Joy and all believers is twofold. First, because of Christ's death on the cross, God does not demand or expect instant perfection. He looks at you as if you were already perfect in Christ. He is gentle and patient with you, giving you all the time you need to grow toward holiness. He, Himself, will make sure the process is completed when Christ returns. Second, even the process of growth in this life is not primarily your responsibility. The Holy Spirit produces growth toward sanctification as we walk in fellowship with Him. The most important thing we can do is to become lovable — to open our hearts, open our lives (including our date books), and receive His love.[19]

In this chapter we have focused on our individual relationship and walk with the Lord. But that is not the whole story. Just as a marriage is lived out in the midst of many relationships — family, friends, and the larger society — that can aid or hinder the growth of the marriage, so also our relationship with God exists in a complex of other relationships both heavenly and human. The next two chapters will explore how these other relationships help and hinder our enjoyment of God.

■ FOR PERSONAL REFLECTION ■

1. What images do the words *holy* and *sanctified* bring to your mind? How accurate are your images to the actual meaning of these biblical terms?

2. Do you ever have the sense that God is proud of you? When does that usually take place?
3. In what ways do you feel your relationship with God is like a marriage relationship? In what ways is it different?
4. Are you filled with the Holy Spirit right now? Why or why not? If not, what would you have to do in order to be filled?
5. What is the relationship between being filled with the Spirit and pursuing Christian maturity?

■ GROUP DISCUSSION GUIDE ■

1. Testimonies: In groups of two to four, have each person briefly share how he became a Christian (if it was too early in life for him to remember, have him tell a significant turning point in his walk or growth). Also, have each person tell how she felt the first few days or weeks of her walk with God (joyful, peaceful, excited, and so on).
2. Can any of you identify with Joy (feeling frustrated and hopeless when confronted with God's demands for perfection)? Do you know any believers who are a little like Joy?
3. In what ways (if any) has reading this chapter changed the way you view the Christian life or your walk with God?
4. In what ways is our walk with Christ similar to (and different from) a marriage relationship?
5. What might be some practical ways this group could help each of us to walk more consistently with and grow closer to God?

■ RECOMMENDED READING ■

Jerry Bridges, *The Discipline of Grace: God's Role and Our Role in the Pursuit of Holiness* (Colorado Springs, Colo.: Nav-Press, 1994). In this challenging but encouraging book, Navigator Bridges explores the role of grace in our growth toward holiness. Intermediate.

Bill Bright, ***The Holy Spirit: The Key to Supernatural Living***
(San Bernardino, Calif.: Here's Life, 1980). A practical guide
to being filled and walking in the Spirit by the founder of
Campus Crusade for Christ. It also includes sections on spiritual warfare and the fruit of the Spirit. Beginning.

Dieter, Hoekema, et. al., ***Five Views on Sanctification*** (Grand
Rapids, Mich.: Zondervan, 1987). An excellent presentation
from advocates of five perspectives on the Christian life
(Wesleyan, Reformed, Pentecostal, Keswick, and dispensational). Each writer presents his own view and then the
others respond. Intermediate.

Charles Caldwell Ryrie, ***Balancing the Christian Life*** (Chicago:
Moody, 1969). This is a classic that is both biblical and practical. Intermediate.

Tim Stafford, ***Knowing the Face of God*** (Colorado Springs,
Colo.: NavPress, 1996). This is an in-depth, realistic exam-
ination of what it means to have a personal relationship with
God. Intermediate.

Michael J. Wilkins, ***In His Image: Reflecting Christ in Everyday
Life*** (Colorado Springs, Colo.: NavPress, 1997). This Talbot
New Testament professor explains the process by which we
become conformed to Christ's image. Intermediate.

CHAPTER ELEVEN

THE INVISIBLE WAR: OUR SUPERNATURAL ALLIES AND ENEMIES

THE SUPERNATURAL IS IN AGAIN. TAKE ANGELS, FOR INSTANCE. It has become popular once again to believe in angels. Enter any secular bookstore and you will find an entire rack of paperbacks filled with stories of people who claim to have met, spoken to, and been helped by angelic beings.[1] Movies and television continue to portray angels, often in quite unbiblical ways.

During the past couple of years, I have carried on a periodic correspondence with Roger Ebert, movie critic for the *Chicago Sun Times*. We have traded views on morality, theology, and the movies. Here are some excerpts from one exchange on the nature of angels.

> **Ebert:** Surely the makers of *The Preacher's Wife* do not believe that humans go to heaven and become angels. As we all know, angels were created by God as his first companions, and he created humans

143

much later. . . .

Scholes: Perhaps you meant this comment ironically. I do not think Hollywood filmmakers take their theology from catechisms, serious theological works, or (God forbid) the Bible. Rather, I presume their view of God, angels, the afterlife, and so on, comes mostly from other movies (and perhaps television). The defining example for most filmmakers is, I suppose, *It's a Wonderful Life*, where Clarence, who has yet to earn his wings, is identified as a clock maker who had died two hundred years before.

But I suspect this is not the first example in American film to blur the angelic-human distinction. Do you know of others? Can you tell me the first?

Ebert: Angels have been defined inaccurately ever since the Renaissance, when they were first provided with wings—needless, because they neither live in a place with air nor have bodies. Movies, I suppose, have been wrong since the first.

Scholes: Actually, in the first few centuries A.D., Christian writers toyed with the idea that angels had some kind of airy or fiery bodies, but by the Middle Ages, theologians had concluded that they must be beings of pure spirit (influenced primarily by Hebrews 1:13-14). You may be right that the earliest depiction of winged angels in literature or art did not occur until the Renaissance, but surely these were influenced by the Old Testament. There we find at least two places where beings generally understood as angels are described as having wings (see Isaiah 6:2 and Ezekiel 1:5-9). However, you are quite right that nearly all theologians (Catholic, Orthodox, and Protestant) from the Middle Ages to the present have explained the physical appearance of angels in the

Bible as a somewhat arbitrary form temporarily assumed for the sake of communicating with humans.

Though there is much interest in supernatural beings, there is also much confusion. So let's take a closer look at our invisible allies and enemies.

GOD'S ANGELS: OUR FAITHFUL ALLIES

Roger Ebert is quite right that popular culture has spread considerable misinformation about angels.[2] Angels are a separate class of created being,[3] not good people who have died. God's faithful angels do not fall in love with human beings, much less have sex with them (as some recent movies have portrayed). Since popular media is an unreliable source of information, we will turn to the Bible to discover who angels are and why they exist.[4]

Their Nature: Personal Spirits

The Bible portrays angels as having the characteristics of persons: intellect,[5] emotions,[6] and will.[7] Although they sometimes appear to humans in a physical form,[8] angels' basic nature is spiritual, not physical.[9]

Apparently angels exist in some hierarchy of organization. This should not surprise us because we know that God prefers order, not chaos, in His church.[10] If all of His other creations are intricately designed and ordered, it makes sense that His unfallen servants also would be organized in some orderly fashion. Although we don't know the exact classifications in detail, we uncover some tantalizing glimpses of the angelic structure in Scripture. The highest angels are called archangels. Although Michael is the only one of the group whose name we are given,[11] it's likely there are others, because Michael is called "one of the chief princes."[12]

At least two classes of angels appear in the Bible: cherubim[13] and seraphim.[14] We do not know how these may be related to each other or to other possible groups of angels.[15] It seems likely there may be more classes of angels not explicitly named in Scripture because Revelation tells us there are "myriads of myriads, and thousands of thousands" (an uncountable number) of angels.[16]

Their Purpose: Ministry

Why do angels exist? What is their purpose? Hebrews 1:14 calls them "ministering spirits." All the roles we see good angels performing in the Bible involve ministering either to individuals or to groups. Specifically, they minister . . .

To God. We would be wrong to think that angels exist only for our benefit. One of their primary roles, perhaps their most important role, is to minister to God Himself. Angels surround God's throne, where they praise and worship both the Father and the Son.[17] They serve God[18] and rejoice in His creation.[19]

To the nations. The archangel Michael seems to have a special role as guardian of the nation of Israel.[20] Persia and Greece also are named as countries under the care of particular angels.[21] It may be that every country has a guardian angel. But the angelic ministry to the nations will not always be one of protection. We are told there will come a time when angels will be the agents of God's judgment on the nations.[22] Even in our own era, angels may be tools of God's judgment against ungodly leaders.[23]

To Christ. From Christ's birth to His resurrection, angels surrounded and ministered to our Lord during His life on earth. Angels announced His birth to shepherds,[24] warned Joseph to flee when Christ was a baby,[25] ministered to Him after His temptation by Satan,[26] and stood ready to defend Him.[27] Angels strengthened Christ after His agony in the garden[28] and rolled away the stone at His resurrection.[29]

To believers. Angels are sent to render service for the sake of believers.[30] They may be God's agents to answer prayers.[31] They can bring messages of encouragement.[32]

I am commonly asked, "Does every believer have one particular guardian angel?" Nowhere does the Bible clearly state this. Yet it may well be that every believer has more than one angel guarding and assisting him or her.[33]

Occasionally God works directly, without intermediaries or go-betweens. When God miraculously heals in answer to prayer, when we are saved through the regeneration of the Holy Spirit, or when we hear God speak in a "still small voice,"[34] it is a direct action of God. But God often works His will through intermediaries such as His good angels. I have called them God's "secret agents" because most of their work is unseen by humans, and I suspect they like it that way. Even if we think that an angel was instrumental in accomplishing God's purpose in our lives, we should thank God as the ultimate source of our aid.[35]

In the book of Job, Satan complains that God has "put a hedge" around Job, his family, and everything Job owned.[36] Although the passage does not say so, I think much of that "hedge" consisted of angels who guarded and protected Job and all that was dear to him. It is likely that God has a similar "hedge" of angels around you and every other believer. This doesn't mean that tragedy will never strike you (as Job discovered). It does mean, however, that any pain and suffering you experience as a Christian can only occur with God's knowledge and specific permission.

Six weeks ago I was driving in rush-hour traffic on one of the congested freeways here in southern California. As the line of cars in front of me suddenly slowed and I slammed on my own brakes, a tow truck rammed me from the rear, shoving me into the three cars in front. My own car was totaled. When my wife saw it a few days later, it was all she could do to hold back tears as she imagined how close she had come to being a widow. I escaped with some internal bleeding around the waist where the seat belt caught me, a concussion, and some damage to my inner ear. Most days since then I have experienced mild to moderate dizziness. Even as I write these lines, I have to stop every few minutes to let the dizziness pass. I'm not safe to drive a car, and the doctor says this could go on for months.[37]

What happened? Did the tow truck catch my "freeway angels" by surprise? I don't believe so. I imagine the angels were right there and may be the explanation for why I'm here at my computer instead of dead.[38] While God does not wish evil for any of His children and often sends His angels to prevent or lessen it, their presence is not a guarantee that no harm will ever come to us. But the knowledge that I am continually surrounded by God's angels is a great comfort to me. It is another expression of how much God loves and cares for me every day.

Yet God's faithful angels are not the only supernatural forces in the unseen world that surrounds us. Let's take a glimpse into that dark side of the angelic realm and learn the truth about Satan and his demons.

SATAN AND DEMONS: OUR AWESOME ENEMIES

Many people today believe in the existence of good angels but tend to discount or find incredible the idea that there might be evil angels, such as demons and Satan. But for me, the opposite was true—I came to believe in the evil angels first.

The year was 1967. The place was the Forum coffee house on Telegraph Avenue, a short stroll from the University of California at Berkeley campus. For a few days in January, this hangout for artists, street people, and drug dealers had been taken over by Christians to share the good news of Jesus Christ with the Berkeley counter-culture.[39] Lambert Dolphin was going to be speaking early in the week. Because I had prayed with him to receive Christ less than two months before, Lambert asked me to sing a few folk songs and share a brief testimony before he gave his message.

At that point in my life, however, I really had very little to say about the gospel. I knew that God was real and that I had met Him. I knew that Christ had made possible my new relationship with God, but I had not yet confronted the question of the reality of angels and demons. If you had asked me about this issue, I probably would have said something about unconscious projection or a prescientific world view.

We arrived at the coffee house about an hour before Lambert and I were scheduled to speak. It was still early on a typically warm California winter evening. There was lots of activity on the street as I walked to the front door of the coffee house. It looked like the beginning of an impromptu street festival with vendors, musicians, and people in brightly colored clothing beginning to dance.[40]

Lambert guided me into a small room behind the informal stage and closed the door.

"It's time to bind the Evil One," he said. I had no idea what he meant; I had never heard the expression before.[41]

"Our awesome God and Father," Lambert prayed in his normally booming voice, as I wondered if the kitchen help in the next room could hear. "We pray that the blood of Your Son would bathe this coffee house. Prevent Satan and his demons from even entering the room. Let the truth of Your gospel soar unhindered in this place."

Listening, I felt torn. I respected and admired Lambert for his boldness and his kindness to me and others. But could this trained scientist really believe in little guys with horns, tails, and pitchforks flying around in red pajamas?[42]

He finished praying, and we reentered the main room. It was time for me to sing and for Lambert to speak. The audience sat quietly, drank strong coffee, and listened. When it was over, I spoke briefly to a few people and then walked through the smoke-filled room and out the front door.

As I passed through, the contrast between the coffee house and the street hit me with a force that was almost physical. The street festival was now in full swing. Men and women in painted faces and scant, gaudy clothes leered at each other and me with drug-glazed eyes. Guitars, tambourines, and bongos throbbed, and dancers whirled with a kind of frenzy I had never seen. They looked almost (the word entered my mind reluctantly) possessed.

I wondered if I might be imagining or exaggerating the difference between the coffee house and the street. I looked back at the open door. People walked freely in and out. I walked slowly back through the door myself. The change in atmosphere was palpable. Inside people sat in pairs or small groups discussing Lambert's message or reading through the *Four Spiritual Laws* booklet. The feeling was peaceful, rational, almost contemplative. But outside the frenetic agitation escalated in a way that was both exhilarating and frightening. I stood for several minutes just inside the door and watched people entering the room. I could see their expressions and even their body posture change as they walked through the door. Shoulders came down as tension flowed away. A cautiously curious look lit their eyes as they looked around the room.

It was clear to me then, as it is now, that a malevolent and very personal power was freely at work in the street but kept out of the room. I suddenly had no doubt that God had answered Lambert's prayer and that the door through which I so easily passed was barred to an evil presence who was desperately seeking to enter.

Satan, the Father of Lies

If you are a Christian who has not yet had any real personal encounter with Satan or demons, you might be tempted (as I was) to dismiss these creatures as the product of some prescientific mythology. However, if you believe Christ is God and therefore cannot lie, and if you believe the Bible accurately records Jesus' words, then you cannot seriously doubt the existence of Satan and demons. Jesus spoke of them as real on numerous occasions.[43] In addition, He met and spoke to Satan in a real, personal encounter.[44] So it's essential to find out as much as we can about the Devil.

His nature. Satan was originally a being of light,[45] a member of the order of angels called cherubim.[46] He may well have been the highest created being in the universe.[47] Even in his current fallen state, Satan retains great power and intelligence. He is called the "god of this world"[48] and "the prince of the power of the air."[49]

Satan is intelligent,[50] has feelings,[51] and possesses a will.[52] Though his intelligence and power are greater than any human's, perhaps greater than any created being's, Satan is finite and does not possess the infinite attributes that belong to God alone. He does not know everything; he cannot be everywhere at once; and he has limitations on his power. In fact, only with the permission of God can he exercise the powers he does possess.[53]

His purpose. Satan's original purpose, like that of all good angels, was to glorify and serve God.[54] But he chose to exercise his free will, turn his back on God's purpose for him, and attempt to exalt himself to the level of God or even higher.[55] Now he lives to destroy, counterfeit, or warp the good things God has created. His eventual hope is that he may pull worship away from God and toward himself.[56] He tries to blind nonbelievers so they cannot hear the gospel.[57] If they do hear the truth, he tries to snatch it away before they can respond with true faith.[58] When a person does receive Christ, he or she now becomes a serious threat to Satan's plans, and so he steps up his attacks. He will try to lure believers into dishonesty[59] or sexual immorality.[60]

Satan's Demon Horde

Because Satan can't be everywhere at once, he has demon helpers around the world to do his work for him. Here are some things to know about them.

Their nature. Jesus referred to demons as Satan's angels.[61] They are likely the "third of the stars of heaven" that are mentioned in Revelation 12:4, who followed Satan in his fall.[62] As angels, they have high intelligence and use it to promote a system of false doctrine.[63] Like Satan and other angels, they are finite and can be in only one place at a time.[64]

Their purpose. Demons are under Satan's rule and seek to promote and extend his kingdom in every way possible.[65] Among other things, they will try to hinder God's good angels in bringing answers to prayer.[66] Sometimes they are able to perform supernatural acts (counterfeit miracles).[67] They can bring physical sickness.[68] Together, Satan and demons are engaged in all-out warfare against God and His church.

Their end. The good news is that Satan and his demons will not be free to do their destructive work forever. Jesus foretold their final judgment when He spoke of "the eternal fire which has been prepared for the devil and his angels."[69]

Christians who believe in Satan and demons often seem to fall into two opposite sorts of errors. Some Christians become fascinated with combating the occult and demonic. While it is true that God calls some believers to focus on helping demon-oppressed and possessed individuals, I get worried when I see young believers becoming enamored with that ministry. I am glad that I have not been called to spend much time in direct confrontation with the forces of darkness.

Other believers make the opposite error: they become so fearful of Satan's power that they are neutralized in their possible impact for God's kingdom. Fear and insecurity are two of the enemy's greatest weapons in dealing with Christians.

What is the balance? We should respect Satan's power and intelligence. He is of an order of created being that is higher than us. We should not lightly or foolishly dabble in the occult or casually associate with those who do. On the other hand, we need to remember that Satan and all his forces are no match for the power of Christ, who dwells in us. "Greater is He who is in you than he who is in the world."[70] When confronted by Satan's power, we need to stand up to him in the power and authority of Christ.[71]

The Big Three Enemies

When writing to the church at Ephesus, Paul warned of three enemies those believers would face in their lives: the world, the Devil, and the flesh.[72] We face the same three enemies today, and it is important to know the differences among them.

The world. "The world" refers to the philosophies of the world, nonChristian world-views. The Bible warns us not to love the world[73] or be conformed to it but to be transformed by the renewing of our minds.[74] This means that we need to develop a Christian world-view. We must learn to think God's thoughts after Him—to increasingly see the world and other people as He sees them.

The Devil. We are told to resist him (in God's power), and we are given the assurance that if we do, he will run from us.[75] Our biggest problems in facing Satan (or his demons) are fear of him or interest in what he claims to be able to give us.

The flesh. The flesh is our own fallen, lustful desires. It is that part of us left over from before we were Christians. We should make no provision for our flesh.[76] That is, we should not put ourselves in situations that we know will tempt us. Plan in advance the ways you will avoid temptations, whenever you can. We need to run from lust while chasing righteousness.[77]

Although our three foes are interrelated[78] and often join forces against us,[79] we should distinguish among them and try to discern the source of our temptation whenever possible. The strategies that work against one foe are not necessarily effective against the others. For example, while it is wise to run away from the lusts of the flesh, fleeing the world won't work. It is impossible to run away from a nonChristian world-view and still be of any use to the Lord. We are "in" the world; we just need to learn not to be "of" it. Christ wants us to be sanctified in truth.[80] Likewise, trying to stand up to fleshly temptation and resist it is a sucker's play. We should follow the example of Joseph, who, when faced with sexual temptation from Potiphar's wife, got out of there as fast as his feet would carry him![81] Similarly, while renewing our minds is a good defense against the world, it is useless against Satan. He is smarter than we are and would love to draw us into a debate. Once he has engaged us and has us listening, he is halfway to having us convinced.[82]

What do we do if we cannot discern which enemy we are up against? Fortunately there are two strategies that are always appropriate: using God's Word and turning to prayer.[83]

The Enemy's Strategy—and Ours

Peter warned us to "be of sober spirit, be on the alert. Your adversary, the devil, prowls about like a roaring lion, seeking someone to devour."[84] In many non-Western countries, Satan is quite overt and bold in showing himself and holds millions of people in fear of evil spirits. But in the Western world, our enemy has successfully pursued a different strategy. In the 1700s, Enlightenment philosophers (especially David Hume) argued that the supernatural was impossible. This has had a profound effect on the secular, scientific world-view ever since. During the modern scientific era (beginning at the end of the nineteenth century in the United States, earlier in Europe), an educated person felt foolish admitting belief in angels and especially in devils. This was a brilliant stroke on Satan's part. He gave up a century of belief in himself but gained a population of millions who were unaware of his presence or activity.

As we are entering a postmodern era,[85] there is a renewed interest in and openness to the supernatural, especially in the form of Eastern mysticism and spiritualism (the new age movement). However, now there is an assumption that if a supernatural phenomenon is real, it must be good. A century of disbelief seems to have removed any caution that the supernatural might be real and also dangerous. With many nonbelievers, Satan now has the best of both worlds. They are fascinated by the supernatural but naïve to its possible perils.

Sadly, not only the secular world has been influenced by Satan's strategy. Many Christians continue to be powerfully affected by the world that surrounds them. After being a Christian for more than thirty years, I still find that I am sometimes slow to recognize when I'm in the middle of spiritual warfare.

I wrote the first draft of this chapter on Satan and demons during a Campus Crusade staff-training conference in Fort Collins, Colorado. I was rushing to finish the chapter so that I could give it to my students to read as a part of the Doctrine Survey class I was teaching. I began to write the opening story about Lambert in the coffee house on a Sunday evening. Then I went to bed early because I had to teach the class at eight the next morning. In the middle of the night I woke up with the most violent stomach flu I have ever experienced. I vomited all through the night and was still retching in the shower as I got ready for class. I was so weak that I had to sit down all through my two-hour lecture. I asked the two hundred students to pray for me, then went straight to bed after class and slept until dinner time. By then I was able to eat a little and sit up enough to continue writing. Once I completed the opening story, I experienced no more symptoms.

Could it have been just a coincidence—a bad case of the twelve-hour flu? I don't believe it. Satan has a vested interest in hiding and suppressing the truth about himself.

A month later I was back in California working on the book proposal to send to prospective publishers. I needed to send several excerpts from this book to my longtime friend and literary agent, Janet Grant. I had tried repeatedly for several days to send it via e-mail. The files just got stuck somewhere in cyberspace. Finally, we gave up on e-mail and I began to fax the pages to her. Again and again, over several frustrating hours, the transmission would quit at the top of the same page. Finally I looked closely at that page. It was the same story—Lambert in the coffee house. I called Janet and read her the page that wouldn't transmit. There was a moment of silence on the telephone line. Then Janet said, "I don't want to have anything more to do with this book!" We both started laughing. Then we prayed together and I tried to fax the pages one more time. It still stopped at the beginning of the same page!

A few minutes later, Janet called back. "Guess what?" she said. "I just happened to check my e-mail, and what do I find waiting in my in-basket?—a complete copy of your file. It looks like the first one you tried to send three days ago!"

It frustrates me that praying is often the last thing I think of in situations like that. My twenty years of upbringing in a nonChristian world-view holds a subtle and powerful sway even after more years of being a Christian. My first instinct is still to look for the natural explanation. "It's just a flu bug; the e-mail provider must be down; something's wrong with the file format." Only later do I wake up and realize that my struggle is not against flesh and blood (or things humans have made, like modems and software) "but against the powers, against the world forces of this darkness, against the spiritual forces of wickedness in the heavenly places."[86]

In this chapter we've been looking at spirit beings who help and hinder our walk with and growth in Christ. In the next chapter we take a new look at one of God's most powerful (and often under-used) tools for our growth in grace: His church.

■ FOR PERSONAL REFLECTION ■

1. Have you ever had an experience in which you believe good angels played a part?
2. What misconceptions about angels do people (think about family members, friends, coworkers, and so on) tend to hold?
3. Why do you think God created angels (as opposed to just creating human beings)?
4. Do you have any doubts about the existence of Satan and demons? Why or why not? Are the descriptions of Satan

and demons in this chapter different in any way from the way you've thought about them in the past?

5. In what ways (if any) have your ideas about Satan and demons been influenced by popular media? Which of the two errors about Satan and demons (fear or fascination) are you more likely to fall into? What can you do to maintain balance in your responses to them?

6. Which of the three enemies (world, Devil, and flesh) tend to make the most trouble for you in your Christian life? What is one practical step you could take to begin to do battle with that enemy more effectively?

■ GROUP DISCUSSION GUIDE ■

1. Experience analysis: Has anyone in the group ever had an experience (or heard of an experience) where it seemed like an angel or demon was involved but he or she was not sure if it really was a supernatural being? Have one or two share about such experiences.

2. How can we tell whether our experiences (or those of others) are really supernatural or not? What biblical criteria might we use?

3. Many people who believe in God or even in Christ do not believe in angels or Satan or demons. What difference does it make whether we believe these supernatural beings exist?

4. Why do you think there has been such an increase in interest in angels in recent years? Do you think there has been a corresponding rise in belief in Satan and demons? If so, why is this so?

■ RECOMMENDED READING ■

Neil Anderson, *The Bondage Breaker* (Eugene, Oreg.: Harvest House, 1990). A practical and motivational book that tells how to deal with the demonic through knowing your position in Christ. Beginning.

Donald Grey Barnhouse, *The Invisible War* (Grand Rapids, Mich.: Zondervan, 1965). This still-valuable classic by a famous Presbyterian pastor includes two excellent chapters on the world, the Devil, and the flesh. Intermediate.

C. Fred Dickason, *Angels, Elect and Evil* (Chicago: Moody, 1975). This is an excellent, thorough, biblical introduction to the subject. Intermediate.

Billy Graham, *Angels: God's Secret Agents* (Waco, Tex.: Word, 1986). Graham has given us a popular, sound, and thorough introduction to good angels. Beginning.

Wayne Grudem, *Systematic Theology* (Grand Rapids, Mich.: Zondervan, 1994). Grudem's complete systematic theology contains a brief (fifteen-page) but very good chapter on angels. Intermediate-advanced.

C. S. Lewis, *The Screwtape Letters* (New York: Macmillan, 1943). Lewis provides wonderful insights into the nature of Satan and demons in this classic collection of satirical letters written from a senior devil to a junior tempter. Beginning.

Timothy M. Warner, *Spiritual Warfare: Victory over the Powers of This Dark World* (Wheaton, Ill.: Crossway, 1991). This missions professor from Trinity Evangelical Divinity School gives an excellent basic introduction to the practical side of dealing with demons. Beginning.

CHAPTER TWELVE

THE CHURCH: OUR NEW FAMILY

"IMMORALITY, DIVORCE, DISHONESTY. THE BODY OF CHRIST seems so sick these days. And what feels worse to me as a pastor is that I see a nearly universal apathy toward spiritual things by those in the pew."

The Reverend John Wilson sat across from me in the coffee-shop booth, his eyes and the droop of his shoulders speaking loudly of discouragement and defeat. "I'm beginning to think," he went on, "that it must be widespread demon possession or oppression of church people."

He had told me of leaving his most recent church after ten years in the ministry and starting work as a carpenter to feed his family. I hesitated to speak, knowing the last thing John needed to hear was some sort of pat answer.

"You're right about the desperate problems plaguing the church," I began. "However, I'm not sure that mass exorcism is the answer. I've seen God solve these kinds of problems through the deep fellowship and encouragement that can blossom among members of Christ's body."

"Fellowship" and "encouragement." They seem like such fragile and impotent words in the face of the gale-force winds of confusion and sin that batter today's church. But these two words speak with powerful voices as they resound through the pages of the New Testament. Encouragement was a dynamic force for change in the early church, and fellowship (as one pastor put it) "was a lot more than red punch and stale cookies!"

The most frequently used New Testament word translated "fellowship" is *koinonia,* which means "communion, fellowship, sharing in common."[1] The basis for our fellowship with other believers is the fellowship *(koinonia)* we each have with God the Father,[2] Son,[3] and Holy Spirit.[4] So our fellowship with one another should be a reflection of the love relationship we have with our Lord.[5]

GATHERED FOR THREE PURPOSES

The New Testament word for church, *ekklesia,* simply means a gathering or assembly. But why do we gather? An assembly for what purpose? God has called the church to three broad purposes: exaltation, edification, and evangelism. I will talk about the church's role in edification and evangelism later in this chapter, but for now I would like to focus on what I believe is our single greatest calling and privilege as believers.

Exalt: Lift God in Worship

I noticed a couple of new faces in our Sunday morning service and went over to introduce myself.

"Are you new to the area?" I asked.

"Naw, we've lived here about ten years," the wife said. "We've tried most of the churches around but we just can't seem to find one that suits us."

"Where did you attend most recently?" I asked.

She told me the name of the church.

"I've heard that's a good church," I said.

"I guess so," she said. "There were some things we liked about it, but . . . well . . ." She looked at her husband.

"We just didn't get very much out of the worship," he added.

I was tempted to ask, "What do you think God got out of it?" But because I had just met them, I decided to hold my peace. Yet I'm afraid this couple represents a trend that is all too common among Western Christians. We go to a church as long as it seems to meet our needs. Then we find something we don't like about the service and move on, looking for one we like better.

I think part of the problem is that we have lost sight of the meaning and purpose of worship. We need to take a closer look at the concept of worship and the reasons why we should worship.

Worship is lifting Him up. The Bible tells us repeatedly that we are to "exalt" the Lord. King David sang, "O magnify the LORD with me, and let us exalt His name together."[6] Isaiah wrote, "O LORD, you are my God; I will exalt you and praise your name, for in perfect faithfulness you have done marvelous things."[7] "Exalt" simply means to "lift up." To exalt God means to place Him in a position of high honor and praise. Our marvelous Lord—who He is and what He has done—should be the center of our worship times as a body. The minister is not the center. The music leader is not the center. The musicians are not the center. The congregation is not even the center. God Himself is (or should be) the center of our worship.[8]

Worship is bowing ourselves down. The most common biblical word translated "worship" literally means "to bow down or prostrate." I must confess there is something deep within me that rebels and resists when I hear that I am to prostrate myself before anyone, even God. We saw in chapter 7 what it is. It is the sin nature that has been with me from birth because of Adam's fall. Satan's own fall came when he tried to exalt himself to be equal with God.[9] This was the same temptation he dangled in front of Adam and Eve when he said, "You can be like God."[10] It is also the temptation our enemy continually puts before the human race today. "Grow up; be proud; assert yourself; make your mark. Don't go groveling to Him like some childish slave. Don't submit your mind and heart to His Word; think for yourself!"[11] So many of us, even as Christians, buy into the lie that the way to get ahead is to exalt ourselves.

The truth is, the way up is down. "Humble yourselves in the presence of the Lord, and He will exalt you," James told us.[12] Peter echoed, "Humble yourselves, therefore, under the mighty hand of God, that He may exalt you at the proper time."[13] Where did the disciples get this radical idea? They learned it from Jesus' own words and example. When His followers started squabbling over which of them was the greatest, He told them, "The greatest among you shall be your servant. And whoever exalts himself shall be humbled; and whoever humbles himself shall be exalted."[14]

My problem for much of my life has been that I want Christian character but I don't want to pay the price. I would like humility, but I don't want to go through the experience of being repeatedly humiliated. I want to learn patience, but I don't want to spend time around people who irritate me. I want to know God, but I don't want to spend hours every week kneeling before Him. However, there is no short cut. These experiences are the price of true spiritual progress.

The first reason we should worship the Lord and lift Him up is that so many of the great spiritual heroes of the Bible have told us to do it. But the Bible also presents us with other reasons for worshiping our Lord.

Worship is deserved by God. Perhaps the best reason to worship God is that He is worthy of our worship. In a vision the prophet Isaiah saw God "sitting on a throne, lofty and exalted." Then an angel called out, "Holy, Holy, Holy, is the LORD of hosts, the whole earth is full of His glory."[15] Hundreds of years later, John received a similar vision, but this time the occupant of the throne clearly was the Son. In John's vision, uncounted thousands of angels said, "Worthy is the Lamb that was slain to receive power and riches and wisdom and might and honor and glory and blessing."[16] We should worship God because He is worthy of our worship.

This leads us to another reason.

Worship will be our eternal occupation. Unfortunately, a common caricature of heaven is that we will sit on a cloud all day, sunning our wings and playing harps. In the final chapter of this book I will try to show how faulty a picture that is. For now I simply want to point out that whatever else eternal life involves, it will surely include a significant amount of time worshiping God. In both of John's visions of God's throne, human believers, as well as angels, engage in continual praise and worship.[17] I believe this will be the most thrilling, challenging, and rewarding work any human has ever attempted: to grow — individually and together — toward the goal of adequately honoring the infinite, eternal God. The sooner we get serious about learning how to do this well, the better!

Worship is a wise use of time. A common complaint of many American Christians is "I'd like to spend more time in worship, but I'm just too busy. I have to earn a living, spend time with my spouse and kids, teach Sunday school, and sit on three committees. There's not much time left for worship." When Paul wrote to the Ephesians, he put a slightly different spin on the issue of time and priorities. He warned them, "Be careful how you walk, not as unwise men, but as wise, making the most of your time, because the days are evil."[18]

So Paul was warning us that when we are in evil days (I think our current era qualifies), we need to keep our priorities clear and make the best use of our time. I've heard these verses quoted as a proof text for evangelism, financial giving, and missionary service, among other causes. However, recently I noticed that none of these worthy enterprises is actually discussed in the immediate biblical context. Rather, Paul went on to up the ante by saying, "So then do not be foolish, but understand what the will of the Lord is."[19] So this is not just friendly advice from cousin Paul; now he's talking about God's will for us. And what is God's will for us? What should be the priority in evil days? He says we should not get drunk (an obvious time waster) but "be filled with the Spirit, speaking to one another in psalms and hymns and spiritual songs, singing and making melody with your heart to the Lord." In other words, worship![20]

Worship is a gift to God. Have you ever pondered the wonderful gifts God has given us? He gave us life itself. He gave us a beautiful world in which to live. He gave us other humans made in His image to know and love. Finally, He gave us the greatest gift: the gift of His only Son to die in our place so He could bring us back into an unbreakable relationship with Himself. Have you ever wished you could adequately thank Him? Have you ever wished there were some gift you could give Him in return? The writer to the Hebrews was pondering these gifts (particularly our permanent position in Christ). His conclusion was "Let us show gratitude, by which we may offer to God an acceptable service with reverence and awe."[21] You already possess a gift you can give back to God every day for the rest of eternity; it's the gift of your thanksgiving, praise, and worship.

In addition to all these reasons, I'd like to mention one final motivation for worship.

Worship is a chance to feel God smile![22] Does it fit your image of God to visualize Him smiling at you? The prophets spoke directly of the joy God takes in His people. "The LORD your God is with you, he is mighty to save. He will take great delight in you, he will quiet you with his love, he will rejoice over you with singing."[23] I think it is reasonable to conclude that one of the things that brings God's heart the greatest joy is the worship of His people.

For me, this is one of the most powerful reasons to worship. It brings me joy to know that I am bringing joy to God as I worship Him. The Westminster Larger Catechism has it right: "Man's chief and highest end is to glorify God, and fully to enjoy

Him forever."[24] This is one of the primary keys to enjoying God: to learn to enter into His joy as we worship.[25]

Now perhaps you can see why I was tempted to ask the new couple in our church what God got out of the worship. When we come together as the body of Christ to worship, it is not primarily for our benefit (though true worship does have the side effect of blessing the worshipers). We come together for worship in order to bring joy to God. So this is the first purpose of the church, to lift God in worship. The other two purposes of the church do exist to benefit other people, both believers and nonbelievers.

Edify: Build Up the Body

All of us who know Christ are called to edify (build up) His body, but frequently we busy Western Christians simply do not invest the time to really build or be built up. Yet God intends us to minister to each other, as members of the body of Christ, in several ways.

Through genuine fellowship. When my wife, Jan, and I were first married, our church involvement was like that of many American Christians. We attended Sunday morning worship, occasionally rose in time for Sunday school, and always hurried home so we could eat lunch in front of the television and watch the ball game.

Then, after several years, we moved and joined a church that emphasized small groups. We ended up in a home fellowship with five other couples who met for two and a half hours each week for nearly four years. This was our first real experience together of what it means to be edified in the context of a local church. During the first year, we began to experience genuine New Testament *koinonia* in several tangible ways. For example, we baby-sat each other's kids (even when it wasn't convenient), we brought in meals when someone was sick, we passed maternity and baby clothes from one family to another, we kept a couple's furniture in our garage for six months, and we had regular work days at each other's homes (one time the whole group helped wallpaper our bedroom). These couples became our best friends and grew to be like our extended family.

With dynamic encouragement. Another aspect of our experience during the group's first phase can best be described as "encouragement." A Greek word that is frequently translated "encourage" or "encouragement" in modern translations (often "comfort" or "consolation" in the *King James Version*) is *parakaleo*. It comes from two Greek roots: *para,* which means "by the side," and *kaleo,* which is the verb "to call." It literally means "to be called alongside." The ministry of encouragement or "being called alongside" is one for which God has called, commissioned, and equipped every Christian.

"Therefore encourage one another, and build up one another, just as you also are doing."[26] Amazingly, this is the same Greek word Jesus used when promising the Holy Spirit. "I will pray the Father, and He shall give you another Comforter, that he may abide with you for ever."[27] God has called us to be to each other what the Holy Spirit is: a comforter and encourager.

Every week our group would take up to an hour to share what had been happening in each of our lives and to pray for each other. We had only two "rules." First, each of us would make it a high priority to come each week unless we were sick or out of town. Second, anything that we said in the group was confidential and not to be repeated outside without explicit permission. In time these commitments built a warmth and trust that paved the way for us to enter the second phase of New Testament encouragement: loving accountability.

By transforming accountability. The word *parakaleo* is also often translated "exhort." "Exhort one another daily."[28] Moving toward a ministry of exhortation and accountability was possible only because we had spent many months in the caring and encouraging of "phase one" fellowship. As David Augsburger says in *Caring Enough to Confront:*

Building solidarity in relationships with others (through caring, support, empathy, trust, affirmation, understanding and love) provides a foundation for the more powerful actions of confrontation, criticism, evaluation, counsel, assertiveness, disagreement and open leveling with each other.[29]

During the second year, one couple, Robert and Helen, began tentatively to share their marital tensions and frustrations. Bob was a college professor and loved to spend his evenings and weekends poring over professional journals, leaving little time for his family. One day Helen told my wife, Jan, "If we weren't Christians, I'd have divorced him by now. Even so, I'm not sure how much more I can stand!"

At this point the group stepped in. The other men insisted that Bob pay for a baby-sitter one night each week and take Helen out for coffee and dessert just to talk. We also urged him to set aside every Saturday morning to spend undivided time with his three kids. Bob responded, "I really don't know what to do with them; everything they like to do is so childish!" So for a couple of Saturdays following that meeting, our family went with his family to the park so Bob could see how I "had fun with the kids."

A year and a half later Helen told Jan that the group "saved their marriage." Now Robert and Helen are in a parachurch ministry, where part of their work is marriage and family counseling.

Our own family was by no means exempt from the group's loving accountability. The men got after me for not keeping our lawn mowed, and one even regularly lent me his power mower so I would have no excuse! And, more seriously, they dealt with my habit of running up credit-card bills I couldn't pay. This time it was Bob who "came alongside" to help me set up a budget and make certain I stuck to it. Within a year we were out of debt and well on the road to more responsible financial management.

Through godly leadership. The way I have told the story of our experience in small groups, you might imagine that our original group just "fell" together. That was far from the case. In fact, there was an elder in that church who had made it his ministry for many years to form and nurture small groups. He personally met with every new church member and talked about his or her level of interest in being in a small group. He would try to put people in groups with others who shared similar interests, levels of commitment, and life situations. For example, each of the couples in our original group had small children, so we all immediately had many things in common. When early attempts failed, he persevered. Our group of six couples was actually re-formed by him out of the remnants of two other groups that had met briefly and disbanded when several couples decided that groups just "weren't for them." But on the third try, our group of twelve clicked and continued for four years.

No church prospers without called, gifted, dedicated leaders who will selflessly and sacrificially serve the body. The New Testament says a great deal about two types of leaders: elders and deacons. Paul listed detailed qualifications for elders in both 1 Timothy 3 and Titus 1. Among other things, an elder must be monogamous, hospitable, a good teacher, free of addiction, a good household manager, a mature Christian, respected by nonbelievers, not easily angered, and self-controlled.

Similarly, Paul also listed qualifications for deacons in 1 Timothy 3:8-12. The word means "servant," but it is significant that the list of qualifications for deacons is so similar to that for elders.[30] One of the few notable exceptions is that Paul said an elder must be "able to teach,"[31] whereas no such qualification is listed for one to be a deacon. Interestingly, there is one qualification listed for deacons that is nowhere repeated for elders. Paul said deacons must not be "double-tongued" (1 Timothy 3:8), perhaps indicating that deacons have more contact with individual believers and so must avoid the temptation to be "people-pleasers," telling each person what he or she wishes to hear.[32]

Although Paul mentioned the gift of pastor-teacher in Ephesians 4:11, the Bible never directly teaches that someone with this gift should be the sole or primary leader of a local congregation. The origin of this practice in modern evangelicalism is probably a carry-over into Protestantism of the Catholic and Anglican role of a parish priest.[33]

Evangelism: Sharing the Good News

The other responsibility God has given to the church is that of evangelism. Our English term comes from the Greek word meaning "good news." Jesus' commission to "be My witnesses . . . to the remotest part of the earth" (Acts 1:8) was given to the disciples who began the first-century church. There are at least two dimensions to the priority of evangelism for the local church. First, the local church is responsible for taking the gospel to its own local community. Second, every local congregation should be involved in supporting the task of world evangelization. This can be accomplished partly by encouraging and financially supporting local members to heed God's call to go to other countries and cultures. The cause of world evangelization also may lead the local church to support denominational and/or parachurch mission agencies.

While all the subjects discussed in this chapter on the church are important, none of them, in my view, is crucial to the doctrine of salvation and none of them must be believed in order for someone to become a Christian. Therefore, I consider the teachings in this chapter to be either persuasions or opinions.[34]

Many American Christians are tempted to dismiss the local church as hopeless, much as our pastor friend, John Wilson, was close to doing. It often seems to be so much less than it was in the first century, and so much less than God wants it to be now. Whenever I am tempted to doubt the value of the church, I remember how our Lord feels about her and the certain hope He holds for her future. Paul informed us that Christ "loved the church and gave Himself up for her; . . . that He might present to Himself the church in all her glory, having no spot or wrinkle or any such thing; but that she should be holy and blameless."[35]

Every once in a while, I catch a glimpse of the power and beauty of His church the way He means her to be. Shortly after our coffee shop conversation, Rev. Wilson and his family began attending the "house church" where my wife and I worshiped on Sunday evenings (one of six into which our larger congregation was divided). After more than a year of fellowship, encouragement, and prayer, the Wilsons felt ready to reenter full-time ministry. A few weeks before he left to be senior pastor of a church in another state, John told the dozen or so present at the house church, "If it had not been for all of you, I'm not sure we would have made it this last year. We have learned so much from you about true fellowship and encouragement. You have given us a new vision for ministry."

■ FOR PERSONAL REFLECTION ■

1. What is your basic attitude toward the organized, local church? What experiences have influenced your attitude (positively or negatively)?
2. What would you have to see or experience to be more enthusiastic about being involved in your local church than you are now?
3. What is your primary motivation when you attend worship services? Based on your reading of this chapter, what *should* it be?
4. Have any of the points in this chapter increased your motivation? Which ones, and why?
5. Have you ever been a part of a dynamic small group? Are you now? If not, what steps could you take to become a part of one?

■ GROUP DISCUSSION GUIDE ■

1. Group sharing: Have three or four people tell about one of their most meaningful experiences in worship. What made it so special?

2. In which of the three purposes of the church (exaltation, edification, and evangelism) do you feel your own local church is strongest? In which is it weakest?
3. What are some practical ways you feel your own local church could be strengthened in one of these areas?
4. What specific constructive steps could some members of this group take this week to help their local church grow stronger?

■ RECOMMENDED READING ■

Paul Enns, *The Moody Handbook of Theology* (Chicago: Moody, 1989). Enns gives an excellent overview of the entire doctrine of ecclesiology in chapter 25, including a brief discussion of worship. Intermediate.

Wayne Grudem, *Systematic Theology* (Grand Rapids, Mich.: Zondervan, 1994), pages 1003–1015. This is one of the few recent evangelical systematic theologies to include a significant discussion of worship. Intermediate-advanced.

Roberta Hestenes, *Using the Bible in Groups* (Philadelphia: Westminster, 1983). This hundred-page volume is the best thing I've seen on small groups. Chapter 2 on covenants and contracting alone is worth the modest price. Beginning.

Neal F. McBride, *How to Have Great Small-Group Meetings* (Colorado Springs, Colo.: NavPress, 1997). A readable, practical guide to better groups. Also valuable are McBride's *How to Build a Small-Groups Ministry* and *How to Lead Small Groups*. Beginning.

Mark McCloskey, *Tell It Often, Tell It Well* (Nashville, Tenn.: Nelson, 1995). A long-time Campus Crusade for Christ staff member makes a strong case for initiative evangelism. Intermediate.

John Piper, *The Pleasures of God* (Portland, Ore.: Multnomah, 1991). Piper explores what brings gladness to the heart of God. Particularly helpful is chapter 8 about the pleasure God takes in our prayers. Intermediate.

CHAPTER THIRTEEN

LAST THINGS: WHEN WE SEE HIM FACE TO FACE

"DAD, DO YOU EXPERIENCE GOD IN AN INTIMATE WAY?"

My son, Rich, and I were riding in the car. Though he was now in his last year of college, he had that thoughtful look I had seen so often as he was growing up.

"I mean, do you really sense His presence ever? Or often?"

His voice trailed off and the silence in the front seat seemed endless. I so wanted my son to respect and admire me. I wanted to say, "Yes. Of course. All the time." But the sad truth is, there is much that I do not understand about God. And even what I understand is far more than I consistently experience.

"I've had some vivid and intimate times with God," I told my son. "But most of the time it is 'through a glass, darkly.'" In my frustration and desire to know God better, I often have found comfort in Paul's words to the Corinthians: "Now we see through a glass, darkly; but then face to face: now I know in part; but then shall I know even as also I am known."[1] What a promise! Someday I will know God as clearly and intimately as He now knows me.[2]

I ended the first chapter of this book by telling how, as a young Christian, I did not want Jesus to return. I wanted to experience marriage, children, and travel. Now, more than thirty years later, I have done all those things. Even though much of my life has been a wonderful adventure, my perspective has changed; I now long for Jesus to return and for me to be with Him.

No fair, you may be thinking. *You've already gotten to do all the things you wanted. No wonder you're ready to go!* But more has happened to me than simply fulfilling some of my adolescent ambitions. I have begun to catch a faint glimpse of the incredible future Christ has planned for each of us who know Him. Paul told the Corinthian believers that no eye has seen, no ear has heard, no mind has conceived what God has prepared for those who love him.[3]

What We Know for Sure

Because much of what the Bible has to say about the future comes to us through symbols, Christians have often disagreed about the details of what—and when—things are going to happen. But virtually all believers agree on five broad themes concerning our future.[4]

1. Individual life after death. Jesus Himself argued that every person will eventually be raised from the dead,[5] and His followers continued to believe and teach this idea.[6]

2. A real hell and heaven. Jesus frequently spoke of a real hell and described it as a place of torment.[7] He and His followers also taught about a real heaven that Christ was preparing for those who trust in Him.[8]

3. Christ's return to the earth. Even as Jesus was physically departing our planet two thousand years ago, God gave His followers the promise that Jesus will someday return in the same way He left.[9] Nearly all believers through the centuries have understood this to mean a literal event and that He will return in a body that is just as fully physical as the one He had during His resurrection appearances.[10]

4. Final justice for all. Eventually all personal beings, both angels and humans, will be held accountable for what they have done. People who have ignored or rejected Christ's gift of salvation will be judged by their actions throughout life and will all be found guilty.[11] Believers will appear before Christ and be rewarded based on their obedience and devotion to Him.[12] Ultimately Satan and his followers will suffer eternal punishment in the lake of fire.[13]

5. An eternal new order. There will come a time when God will make a new heaven and earth. Believers, now free from all effects of sin, will live in joy, peace, and intimate fellowship with Christ forever.

We will come back to a fuller discussion of some of these things on which Christians agree.[14] But first I want to examine some areas where sincere Christians differ regarding the future of the human race and the world.

THREE VIEWS OF THE LAST TIMES

The primary disagreement among Christians who take the Bible as the final authority on these things concerns the timing of Christ's return in relation to other predicted events. The core of the controversy is the period called the Millennium. Six times in six verses John spoke about a period of a "thousand years" in Revelation 20.[15] During this time Satan will be bound and kept from deceiving the nations while a group of persecuted and martyred believers will reign with Christ. At the end of the thousand years, Satan will be released to deceive the nations for a brief period before his final judgment. Following the thousand years, the rest of the dead will be raised for the final judgment.

This is really all that John tells us about the thousand-year period, and it is not explicitly referred to anywhere else in the Bible.[16] So we're left with a sort of mystery. Does Christ return to the earth *before* or *after* this thousand-year period? Or is the thousand years merely a symbol that doesn't refer to a literal period of time at all? These are the three historic positions that Christians have held, and each view continues to have its advocates today.

Is the Thousand Years a Figure of Speech?

Christians who see Revelation 20 as symbolic often are called amillennialists.[17] They do not think John ever intended the phrase "a thousand years" to be taken literally. Revelation is a highly symbolic book, they argue, and many things in it cannot be taken literally.[18] For them, "one thousand" is a number that symbolizes fullness or completeness.

Amillennialists see the Millennium as taking place now, in the church age. Spiritually, a perfect or millennium peace is available now for those who have Christ ruling as the Lord of their lives. In this view of the future, there are really only three significant periods and events: the church age that extends from Christ's first coming until His second, the return of Christ, and the eternal state with the new heaven and earth.

Will Christ Return After the Thousand Years?

Some believers think that Revelation 20 talks about a period of time that will precede Christ's return. Those who hold this view are called postmillennialists.[19] According to the postmillennial view, Christ working through the church will gradually spread the gospel and bring about social reform throughout the world until there will be a long period of relative peace and godliness in all the nations. Though it may begin gradually, this era of peace will be the Millennium.[20] The postmillennial order of events is this: the church age that gradually transitions into the Millennium, the return of Christ, and then the eternal state.

Will Christ Return Before the Thousand Years?

Other believers think Christ will return at the end of the church age and usher in the Millennium. These believers are called premillennialists.[21] Most premillennialists think the church age will be followed by a period called the Tribulation. Christ will return to earth around the time of the tribulational war and set up an earthly millennial kingdom where He will personally rule as king.[22] At the end of the thousand years will come the final judgment and the new heaven and earth. So the order of events in the premillennial view goes like this: the church age, the Tribulation and Christ's return, the Millennium, and the eternal state.[23]

Even among those within the premillennial camp there is some disagreement. While all premillennialists believe that Christ is coming before the thousand years, there is considerable disagreement about when Christ will return in relation to the Tribulation.

Will Christ return *after* the Tribulation? Some premillennialists hold that the believers who are alive at the end of the church age will go through the period of great suffering that Jesus called "a great tribulation, such as has not occurred since the beginning of the world until now, nor ever shall."[24] Because this view teaches that Jesus will come after the time of trouble, it is called "posttribulational premillennialism."[25] These believers think that when Christ returns, those who have died in Him will rise first, immediately followed by the living believers who will be caught up with Him in an event called the Rapture of the church.[26] Then all believers, living and resurrected, will immediately come down with Christ in their new bodies to rule with Him for a thousand years.

Other premillennialists think that Christ will return *before* the Tribulation begins. This view is called "pretribulational premillennialism." In this view Christ will come secretly for the church who will meet Him in the air, return to heaven with Him, and avoid going through the Tribulation period.[27]

Scholes's View: Christ Comes Before the Millennium and the Tribulation

In my opinion, all of the millennial positions have good biblical arguments in their favor. There have been sincere, scholarly advocates for each of the views listed in this chapter. You can hold any of these positions and be truly saved. Further, you can believe any of these schemes (or be uncertain about which is true) and still grow in your faith and honor Christ. Having said that, I want briefly to tell you why I favor the premillennial, pretribulational view. (I hold this belief as a mild persuasion.)

First, I see no evidence (or likelihood) that the world as a whole is getting better through the preaching of the gospel or through Christian societal influence.[28] Jesus' words and those of His followers seem to predict that a time of great trouble, not of universal peace and love, will come just prior to His return (see Matthew 24:15-31). If a millennial era where nearly everyone had accepted Christ immediately precedes His return, why would Jesus ask the question "When the Son of Man comes, will He find faith on the earth?"[29] For these reasons I do not find the postmillennial view convincing.

Second, it's clear to me that Israel is not the church. My own background is Presbyterian, so I am naturally drawn to the traditional amillennial eschatology of most Presbyterian and Reformed thinkers. I like the Calvinist emphasis that we Christians have inherited the promises God gave to Abraham and that in Christ there is "neither Jew nor Greek, there is neither slave nor free man, there is neither male nor female; for you are all one in Christ Jesus."[30] In the typical amillennial view, God has no plans for Israel as a distinct nation or ethnicity, and Israel's reformulation as a sovereign state in 1948 is a historical curiosity but not prophetically significant.

Though the universal and egalitarian feel of amillennialism appeals to me, I have trouble reconciling it with Paul's words in Romans 11:25-29. According to amillennialists, God no longer distinguishes between Israel and the church—the church is the new Israel. But here was Paul, post-Pentecost, writing to the church (he calls them "brethren"), talking about a future time when "all Israel will be saved." According to the amillennialists, the unfulfilled prophecies about Israel will come true spiritually in the church, but Paul quoted Old Testament prophecies as if they will still be literally fulfilled to Israel. So I am left with the premillennial position by default. It is the only view that seems to harmonize all the biblical data.

Third, Christ can come at any time. This is the primary reason I favor the view that Christ will come to rapture the church secretly before the Tribulation. It is a constantly repeated New Testament theme that Christ can come at any time, and no one will be able to accurately predict when. Jesus told His disciples, "Of that day and hour no one knows," and warned them, "For this reason you be ready too; for the Son of Man is coming at an hour when you do not think He will."[31] However, if the post-tribulational view were correct, those alive at the time could quite accurately predict His coming. Because the Tribulation will last seven years, believers could mark their calendars at the beginning and know with precision when Christ would return.[32] So I accept the pretribulational, premillennial view, largely by default, because it is the view that seems to best harmonize everything the Bible has to say on the subject of the timing of Christ's return.

We Can't Second-Guess Him

I also believe that Christ does not want us to attempt to guess exactly when He is going to return. I was reminded of the dangers of trying to second-guess the Lord's timing a few years ago. A young man named Ron came to me quite upset.

"I'm about to graduate from college, and I've been feeling for the past year like God is calling me to go to seminary and prepare for full-time ministry."

"Great," I said. "But you don't seem very happy about it."

Ron sighed. "I was until yesterday."

"What happened yesterday?" I asked.

"I was listening to a preacher on the radio talk about the Second Coming. He gave some very convincing arguments that Christ was coming soon, probably in the next couple of years. He said every Christian should devote every possible moment to telling others about Christ. He said it is our duty to bring as many into the kingdom as possible before it's too late."

"So you're wondering if it's a waste of time to come to seminary?" I asked.

"Sure," he said. "A seminary degree will take several years to complete. What if Christ returns before I finish? I'll have wasted a bunch of time studying that I could have spent sharing my faith."

I smiled. "This may surprise you," I said, "but I don't think Christ is going to give a prize in heaven to the one who most accurately guesses the time of His coming."

"Well, I never supposed there would be an actual prize. . . ."

"My point is this," I said. "Let's suppose you come to seminary, and what you fear happens. On the day before graduation, Christ returns. What do you think He is going to say to you?"

"I . . . I'm not sure. I guess that's my problem."

"I think He'll say to you, 'Well done, good and faithful servant, you have been faithful in the things I called you to do—enter the joy of your Lord.'"[33]

Ron smiled. "You really think so?"

"Yes," I said. "And let's consider the opposite situation. Let's say that God is really calling you to seminary but, out of fear that Christ may soon return, you never go and you just devote all your time to evangelism. And let's say that it is fifty years before He returns. Then what do you suppose He would say to you?"

"Uhh . . . I guess He'd say I blew it!"

"I think His words to you might be like those of the master to the fearful servant in Jesus' parable. I think He might say, 'Why did you bury your talent when you knew I was calling you to develop and multiply it? How much greater influence for me could you have had if you'd sharpened your ministry skills fifty years ago like I told you to!'"

"I never thought about it like that," Ron said.

"A wise minister once gave me a piece of advice," I said. "He told me that we should live as though Jesus was coming tomorrow but plan as though He wasn't coming for another thousand years."

"Okay, Prof," Ron said, grinning. "Then I guess I'm headed for seminary!"

What Difference Does It Make?

I do not believe that biblical prophecy was given for us to make an accurate chart of future history or to guess the exact time of Christ's return. However, prophecy is a major theme of Scripture. Some have estimated that as many as a third of the passages in the Bible contain some prophetic teaching.

Many years ago, the first time I ever taught a course on biblical prophecy, one of my students asked me a question that caught me by surprise. Charlotte was in her thirties, the wife of a career missionary. They had come to our seminary for further study before they returned to the mission field. We had nearly finished our course in eschatology when Charlotte raised her hand with a frustrated look on her face.

"What's the point of all this prophecy anyway? Why do we spend so much time studying what's going to happen in the future if Christians can't agree on how it all works out?"

I think I mumbled something, but the fact was, I didn't have a good answer. Today I believe I can give much better answers to Charlotte's question simply by raising these points:

Our actions matter. As a young Christian, I studied under a man who later became a well-known speaker on the subject of biblical prophecy. It was from him that I first heard that the main purpose of prophecy was to exhort us to holy living. "Nearly every passage of prophecy from Genesis to Revelation," he told us, "is linked to an exhortation as to how we should live our lives."

A typical example would be 2 Peter 3:11. After prophesying the destruction of the earth by fire, Peter said, "Since all these things are to be destroyed in this way, what sort of people ought

you to be in holy conduct and godliness?" His argument is a powerful one. Because everything you own or ever hope to acquire
(even the clothes you are wearing as you read this and the pages
of the book you hold in your hand) will eventually be burned
away, you should put your time and energy into the one thing
you will carry with you forever: your character.

A tragic footnote is that years later I heard that my prophecy
teacher was placed under church discipline for sexual immorality. Instead of submitting to the discipline, he left the church,
moved across town, and began teaching prophecy classes in a
newly opened seminary.

One day one of his students confronted him after class. "How
can you teach in this seminary when you've admitted commit-
ting adultery, are recently divorced, and are still under discipline
from the church you used to pastor?"

I grieved when I heard the answer he gave the student. "I'm
not teaching a Christian marriage class. I'm just teaching about
prophecy!"

Apparently he had forgotten the vital link between prophecy
and holy living. This connection means that no matter how
poor we are, no matter how little our talent or influence as the
world judges such things, each of our decisions every day has a
significance that will last on into eternity.

All wrongs will be righted. The world we live in is not a fair
place. This is sometimes hard for us Western Christians to grasp.
We live in societies whose justice systems still reflect (however
imperfectly) generally biblical values and the critical idea of individual human rights. But most people in most centuries, even most
Christians, have lived in poverty, in repression, and at the whim
of immoral dictators. In the last seventy years we have seen
Hitler's Holocaust, the purges of Lenin and Stalin, and "ethnic
cleansing" in Bosnia and Iraq, to mention just a few of the horrors of this past century. It is a great comfort and reassurance that
God eventually will step in and hold everyone accountable for
what he or she has done.

Rewards will be given. Some Christians, especially those of us who live in countries that value democracy, have trouble accepting the idea of some believers gaining greater rewards than others. For many years this idea bothered me. I felt that if God is fair, then He has to treat all believers exactly the same. But the third chapter of 1 Corinthians, and other passages, speak of some Christians receiving greater rewards than others.[34] Two ways of understanding this idea have helped me make peace with it emotionally.

First, some have suggested that the rewards are in the form of crowns, which we then return to Jesus.[35] In Paul's last letter he told his son in the faith, Timothy, that he was about to die. Then he said, "In the future there is laid up for me the crown of righteousness, which the Lord, the righteous Judge, will award to me on that day; and not only to me, but also to all who have loved His appearing."[36] Clearly part of what motivated Paul to "keep the faith" was the reward (crown) he knew was waiting for him.[37] In Revelation we see a picture of the end times where believers are casting their crowns down in worship before "the one" sitting on the throne.[38] So it may be that the privilege we have is to return our crowns to the Lord, recognizing that every truly good work we did as Christians, we did in His power. Thus the crowns ultimately belong to Him.[39]

The idea is that when we see Christ, our greatest desire will be to have some tangible way to show our love and gratitude to Him. Those who have earned rewards by trusting Him in their earthly lives will have a present to return to Him in worship and love. Those whose works have all been burned up will be like a child who arrives at a birthday party without a present to give to the one being honored.[40] I think this is a possible way to think about what may happen with rewards.

There is a second suggestion concerning the nature of rewards that I like just as well or perhaps even better. This second idea is that our "rewards" are enlarged capacities for worship. That is, as we serve God in this life, as we walk in the Spirit and worship Him, our capacity for love grows. Our "reward" in heaven is that we arrive there with an enlarged ability to do the primary work of eternity, which is to honor and worship God. We are better able to "enjoy Him forever"!

What Heaven Is Like

When my children were young, more than one of them asked, "What is heaven like, Daddy?" It's one of the toughest questions I ever tried to answer. The images in the Bible are not especially helpful to me, even as an adult. I must admit, I do not find the physical description of the holy city in Revelation 21 (streets of gold, walls of jasper) particularly appealing. Oddly, it is what the Bible says will *not* be there that I find most appealing. We are told there will be no more "mourning, or crying, or pain." Every tear will be wiped away and death will be no more.[41]

What has helped me most to envision a little of what heaven may be like is a passage from *The Last Battle,* one of the children's fantasy stories written by C. S. Lewis. In these stories, Narnia, a land of talking animals, is visited by several British children and adults who there meet its ruler, Aslan, an awesome and beautiful lion. In the final book of the series, many are taken by Aslan through a door into yet another world. Then the children look back through the door and watch Aslan bring their beloved Narnia to its end. Later, as they begin to explore the oddly familiar new world, one of the adults speaks to the children:

> Listen, Peter. When Aslan said you could never go back to Narnia, he meant the Narnia you were thinking of. But that was not the real Narnia. That had a beginning and end. It was only a shadow or a copy of the real Narnia, which has always been here and always will be here: just as our own world, England and all, is only a shadow or copy of something in Aslan's real world. You need not mourn over Narnia, Lucy. All of the old Narnia that mattered, all the dear creatures, have been drawn

into the real Narnia through the Door. And of course it is different; as different as a real thing is from a shadow or as waking life is from a dream.

It was the Unicorn who summed up what everyone was feeling. He stamped his right fore-hoof on the ground and neighed and then cried: "I have come home at last! This is my real country! I belong here. This is the land I have been looking for all my life, though I never knew it till now. The reason why we loved the old Narnia is that it sometimes looked a little like this."[42]

It is true that we do not know exactly how the new heaven and earth will look. What we do know is that the One who made the things on this planet we treasure most (including all the people we love) is the architect of the place we will call home forever.

WE WILL LOVE AND BE LOVED FOREVER

Near the end of His time with His disciples, Jesus began to tell them that soon He would have to leave. Sensing their distress at the thought of losing Him, our Lord uttered one of the most beautiful promises in all of the Bible.

"Let not your heart be troubled," He began. "In My Father's house are many dwelling places; if it were not so, I would have told you; for I go to prepare a place for you. And if I go and prepare a place for you, I will come again, and receive you to Myself; that where I am, there you may be also."[43]

The disciples would have intuitively caught a cultural richness in Jesus' words that is more difficult for us to grasp. The "Father's house" would have immediately called up images of a common Middle Eastern custom. When a wealthy man provided for his family, he would first construct an empty frame around a beautiful inner courtyard. He would then finish off only those rooms needed by his family at the time, leaving the rest of the house roofed but unfinished inside. Then as each son was ready to marry, during the time of betrothal, father and son together would choose an apartment around the courtyard, finish it off and decorate it in anticipation of the wedding day. After the feast was over, the groom would proudly bring his bride to the father's house and show her the lovely rooms that would be her home for the rest of her life.

This is the word picture Jesus was drawing for His disciples. Jesus is the Bridegroom who has gone away for a while and is preparing a special place for each of us in the many dwellings within His Father's house. I often have wondered how my rooms will look. I imagine one may be a huge study lined with books from floor to ceiling. The seating will be dark, soft leather and the walls oiled, ancient oak. But then, it may be nothing like that. For Christ knows far better than I what sort of environment will feel like home to me for eternity.

The part that will make it heaven, however, will have nothing to do with decoration. What will make it heaven is that Jesus will be there with me, and He and I will have a depth of fellowship unmarred by my distraction, weakness, and sin.[44] Then I will know God as He really is and hear Him speak to me directly. I finally will be fully and completely human, reflecting Christ's image with clear brilliance. I will possess the full inheritance Christ died to purchase for me. My walk with the Father, Son, and Holy Spirit will no longer be merely by faith. I will take my place beside God's angels, and the redeemed from all the centuries, to bow down and lift the Lord up in a way that brings Him the honor and glory He deserves.

The unspeakable enjoyment of God, which I now feel only in fleeting moments, of which I hear only the echo, which I see "through a glass, darkly" — that joy will be mine from the moment Christ brings me home. The pleasure and enjoyment of God will get better and richer every day, every year, every century, every millennium . . . forever.

■ FOR PERSONAL REFLECTION ■

1. How would you feel if you found out that Christ was going to return next week? Next year? What do your answers tell you about your Christian walk and/or maturity?

2. Do you have any doubts about the five points listed under "What We Know for Sure" (pages 174-175)? How do you feel about those five things being true?

3. Which of the views of the last times do you agree with? Why? At what level of belief do you hold your view?

4. Is biblical prophecy important to you? Why or why not?

5. Are any of your actions motivated by the promise of eternal rewards? Why or why not?

6. What is your favorite picture of heaven? (What do you think your rooms will be like?)

■ GROUP DISCUSSION GUIDE ■

1. Buzz groups: In pairs, list as many wrong ideas about the future as you can that are believed by people in our country. (Have one person in each pair serve as a "scribe" to write a list of the pair's ideas.) After five minutes, have each scribe read the pair's list to everyone.

2. Do you think Christ is going to return in the next few years? Why or why not?

3. How might we live our lives differently if we knew for certain that Christ was going to return one year from today?

4. Which of those same things should we be doing, even though we don't know for sure?

5. What are some practical ways that the Bible's teaching about the future can make a difference in my Christian life this week?

■ RECOMMENDED READING ■

Gleason Archer, et al., *The Rapture: Pre-, Mid-, or Post-Tribulational?* (Grand Rapids, Mich.: Zondervan, 1984). This volume presents clear arguments for the spectrum of views on the timing of the Rapture. Intermediate.

Robert G. Clouse, ed., *The Meaning of the Millennium: Four Views* (Downers Grove, Ill.: InterVarsity, 1977). This volume includes excellent arguments for the four basic millennial positions. Intermediate.

John Jefferson Davis, *Christ's Victorious Kingdom* (Grand Rapids, Mich.: Baker, 1986). Davis argues effectively for the postmillennial view. Intermediate.

Anthony A. Hoekema, *The Bible and the Future* (Grand Rapids, Mich.: Eerdmans, 1979). Reformed theologian Hoekema makes a very good case for the amillennial position. Intermediate.

C. S. Lewis, *The Great Divorce* (New York: Macmillan, 1946). A fictional bus trip from the beginning of hell to the edge of heaven. Lewis artfully uses this device to explore how our desires lead us to heaven or keep us from it. Beginning-intermediate.

C. S. Lewis, *The Last Battle* (New York: Macmillan, 1956). In this children's story, Lewis paints a compelling picture of heaven as the "true Narnia." Beginning.

NOTES

Chapter One—Our Approach: Convictions, Persuasions, and Opinions
1. Matthew 22:36-37. All Scripture quotations, unless otherwise noted, will be from the *New American Standard Bible* (La Habra, Calif.: Lockman Foundation, 1960).
2. C. S. Lewis, *Mere Christianity* (New York: Macmillan, 1952), p. 8.
3. Lewis, *Mere Christianity,* p. 8.
4. Acts 10:1-35. In the first century, Jewish people followed a strict dietary code that was set out in the Jewish Bible (what Christians call the Old Testament). They could not eat pork, and even other meat had to be prepared in a particular fashion (called "kosher"). However, the book of Acts tells us that God Himself made it clear to Peter that, as Christians, even those from a Jewish background did not need to continue to follow the kosher laws in order to be saved and accepted by God. Therefore, Peter began to eat with the Gentile Christians, enjoying even their nonkosher food. Then a strict group of Jews (called Judaizers or "the party of the circumcision") came from Jerusalem teaching that people had to be circumcised and follow the kosher laws to be truly saved. To placate them, Peter stopped eating with the Gentiles. Paul publicly confronted Peter

because Peter's behavior was hypocritical and was confusing the gospel, altering the good news of how people can be saved.

5. Galatians 2:12.

6. Galatians 2:13.

7. Galatians 2:14.

8. John Brown, *An Exposition of the Epistle of Paul the Apostle to the Galatians* (Evansville, Ind.: Sovereign Grace, 1957), pp. 87-88. See also John Eadie, *Commentary on the Epistle of Paul to the Galatians* (Edinburgh: Clark, 1884), p. 156. The phrase "the truth of the gospel" also occurs in Galatians 2:5, where it is used in a nearly identical fashion. Samuel Driver, Alfred Plummer, and Charles Briggs, eds., *A Commentary on the Epistle to the Galatians* (Edinburgh: Clark, 1921). Also, Ernest Burton, A *Critical and Exegetical Commentary on the Epistle to the Galatians*, p. 11. Also, J. B. Lightfoot, *The Epistle of St. Paul to the Galatians* (Grand Rapids, Mich.: Zondervan, 1957), p. 107. Also, F. F. Bruce, *The Epistle to the Galatians* (Grand Rapids, Mich.: Eerdmans, 1982), p. 115.

9. Galatians 2:5.

10. Although the issues Paul dealt with in these epistles include matters of both doctrine and moral behavior, I am only trying to draw out a paradigm for levels of theological belief. Some might argue that what Paul was dealing with in Galatians 2 was strictly, or primarily, an issue of behavior or practice. While it is my view, and that of the theologians I've quoted, that Paul was dealing with a theological issue (salvation by grace through faith), which was being threatened by behavior, it is not necessary to accept my interpretation. Even if Paul was dealing only with behaviors that require discipline, the broader principle can be taken by way of application, that we should not treat all beliefs the same way.

11. By "breaking fellowship," I mean treating a Christian as we would a nonbeliever. We are polite to nonbelievers and carry on conversations with them, but our objective is to bring them to a relationship with Christ. In the same way, we can still be cordial and speak with a believer who stubbornly disagrees on a conviction-level issue. However, we are not to treat him or her as a believer in good standing. Rather, our whole effort should be concentrated on trying to bring about a return to an orthodox stand in this crucial area of doctrine. Church leaders should be willing to engage in the appropriate steps of church discipline with mature believers who persist in believing and teaching errors on conviction-level doctrines (see Matthew 18:15-17).

12. "Persuaded" (Greek, *plerophoreo*) occurs only eight other times

in the New Testament, always carrying the sense of "full assurance" or of being "fully persuaded." In Romans 4:21, Paul described Abraham's great faith in God as "being fully assured that what He had promised, He was able also to perform." In Colossians 2:2 the apostle grieved for the Laodiceans "that their hearts may be encouraged, having been knit together in love, and attaining to all the wealth that comes from the full assurance of understanding." Here Paul's wish was for comfort and unity combined with full assurance (*plerophoreo*).

13. Frederic Godet, *Commentary on St. Paul's Epistle to the Romans* (Edinburgh: Clark, 1883; reprint edition, Grand Rapids, Mich.: Kregel, 1977), p. 456.
14. Romans 14:10.
15. Romans 14:13.
16. William G. T. Shedd, *A Critical and Doctrinal Commentary on the Epistle of St. Paul to the Romans* (New York: Scribner's, 1879), p. 391.
17. Martin Luther, *Lectures on Romans,* trans. and ed. Wilhelm Pauck (Philadelphia: Westminster, 1961), pp. 382-383.
18. Calvin wrote, "Paul refers to questions which disturb minds not yet sufficiently established, or which entangle them in doubts, as contentious. We may, however, widen this phrase to include any thorny and difficult questions which cause disquiet and disturbance to weak consciences without edifying them." John Calvin, *The Epistles of Paul the Apostle to the Romans and to the Thessalonians,* trans. Ross Mackenzie (Grand Rapids, Mich.: Eerdmans, 1973), p. 290.
19. "For whoever judges someone else certainly believes that the one he condemns is doing something that goes against salvation and that he must therefore change his ways. . . . Therefore, as it was foolish then to regard these things as so weighty that one made salvation dependent upon them, meanwhile neglecting faith and love which alone are sufficient for eternal life . . ." Luther, *Lectures,* pp. 382-383.
20. Luther broke with the Roman church over issues crucial to salvation but refused to break with other Protestants over lesser matters. He was willing to develop separate styles of worship and discuss them with other Protestants, which led to maintaining separate spheres of influence. This is a historical example of rigid separation over an issue of conviction, and of separation with mutual tolerance and acceptance regarding issues of persuasion.
21. While this is a book about theological beliefs, not primarily behavioral issues, I think a similar set of levels could be

developed for Christian ethics. That project, however, is beyond the scope of this book.

22. *Thelo* is a common biblical word, appearing more than two hundred times in the Greek New Testament. Frequently it simply means "will" or "would," but sometimes the word takes on the more tentative nuance of a wish or desire.

23. By making this distinction, I am not teaching more than one level of inspiration or inerrancy of the biblical text. I believe that all of Paul's letters are equally inspired by the Holy Spirit and equally without error in the original autographs. While all statements in Scripture are inspired, all do not apply to believers today in the same way. I think the Holy Spirit Himself wanted us to understand the difference between Paul's binding commands and his personal opinions. I will discuss my views on inspiration, inerrancy, and authority further in chapter 5.

24. Matthew 26:39. Another example of *thelo* used to express a wish or desire for something contrary to God's will is found in chapter 14 of 1 Corinthians. Paul wrote, "Now I wish that you all spoke in tongues, but even more that you would prophesy" (verse 5). Here is a theoretical or hypothetical usage of *thelo*. Paul knew that his wish could not be fulfilled, for he had just said, "All do not speak with tongues, do they?" (12:30). He was saying, in effect, "It would be ideal if everyone could have all the gifts, but. . . ." In this case, Paul was expressing a personal wish, even a desire contrary to known fact.

25. Some of the early Christian creeds did function as boundary statements between true and false beliefs, but in modern times many merely serve to distinguish one group of Christians from another.

26. For example, the one-page statement of faith of Campus Crusade for Christ, which I sign annually, contains a number of conviction-level beliefs (the Trinity, the deity of Christ, salvation by grace through faith, and so forth). The statement also includes some persuasion-level beliefs, such as statements about the filling of the Spirit and the inerrancy of Scripture. Because I can fully affirm all of the articles without mental reservation, I can sign the statement even though I see some of the articles as more central to historic Christianity than others. Through the years, CCC has not treated its statement of faith as the dividing line between true and false faith. CCC leaders and staff have frequently cooperated in evangelistic thrusts with believers from various groups and denominations who could not necessarily sign all the articles of our particular boundary statement.

27. John 4:24.

Chapter Two — Our God: The One Who Exists

1. Romans 1:19.
2. Psalm 19:1.
3. I recently received a mailing from the American Humanist Association. (I wonder how I got on that mailing list!) I was intrigued by the outside of the envelope, which asked, "Are you one of the exceptional 8%?" The letter inside quoted a Gallup poll finding that only 8 percent of adult Americans disbelieved in a god of any kind. Even atheists know they are a tiny minority.
4. Romans 1:21.
5. Psalm 14:1; 53:1.
6. Romans 1:22.
7. The work of British scientists Roger Penrose and Stephen Hawking, in the late sixties and early seventies, demonstrated that the other competing theories were not viable. Hawking states, "In the end our work became generally accepted, and nowadays nearly everyone assumes that the universe started with a big bang singularity." Stephen W. Hawking, *A Brief History of Time* (New York: Bantam, 1988), p. 50.
8. William John Cook, "How Old Is the Universe?" *U. S. News and World Report*, August 18-25, 1997, p. 34.
9. Robert Jastrow, *God and the Astronomers* (New York: Norton, 1978), p. 116.
10. The word *teleological* comes from the Greek *telos*, which means "end." The idea is that we see an end or purpose in the workings of nature.
11. Some theologians and philosophers consider this a separate argument, the "anthropological argument." See J. Oliver Buswell, *A Systematic Theology of the Christian Religion* (Grand Rapids, Mich.: Zondervan, 1962), pp. 90-91.
12. From the Greek word *ontos*, which means "being."
13. Kant also argued that nothing can ever be proved to "exist" from pure logic. Only experience (or some line of reasoning derived from experience) can prove whether something exists. (This seems to me just a bias on Kant's part against deductive arguments in general.) I also should mention that the ontological argument cannot be easily defeated by the common objection that the same line of reasoning can be used to prove the existence of a perfect island, a perfect day, or even (as David and Marjorie Haight proposed) a perfectly evil being, that is, Satan. In defense of Anselm, philosophers have pointed out that the same arguments that apply to a necessary being (God) do not automatically apply to contingent beings. Just because the

ontological argument cannot be used to prove the existence of a perfect island, it does not follow that it is invalid to apply it to God.

14. John Hick argues that "mystics within the different traditions do not float free from their cultural conditioning. They are still embodied minds, rooted in their time and place. They bring their Hindu, Buddhist, Jewish, Christian, Muslim, or Sikh sets of ideas and expectations with them on the mystical path and are guided by them towards the kind of experience that their tradition recognizes and leads them to expect." John Hick, *An Interpretation of Religion: Human Responses to the Transcendent* (New Haven, Conn.: Yale University Press, 1989), p. 295.

15. These approaches are appropriate with Mormons because they validate the Book of Mormon with historical evidence and claim the Bible has been wrongly translated.

16. This newest generation of young adults has most often been called "Busters" or "Generation X." I find both these designations denigrating and so try to avoid their use. I usually just call them "the current generation."

17. I find this mistrust of science and logic common throughout the world among those with a Western-style university education.

18. See Kevin Graham Ford, *Jesus for a New Generation: Putting the Gospel in the Language of Xers* (Downers Grove, Ill.: InterVarsity, 1995); Tim Celek and Dieter Zander, *Inside the Soul of a New Generation: Insights and Strategies for Reaching Busters* (Grand Rapids, Mich.: Zondervan, 1996); and Mark Senter III, *The Coming Revolution in Youth Ministry* (Wheaton, Ill.: Victor, 1992).

19. Bud was a pioneer missionary with Campus Crusade who opened and directed its early ministries in both western and eastern Europe and in the Soviet Union.

20. Years later I realized that what he was drawing on the napkin must have been an early, memorized version of the Four Spiritual Laws.

21. Stephen Davis writes, "One could almost say that debate about the existence of God is a consuming passion of twentieth-century philosophers of religion." Stephen T. Davis, "What Good Are Theistic Proofs?" in *Philosophy of Religion: An Anthology*, Louis P. Pojman, ed. (Belmont, Calif.: Wadsworth, 1987), p. 80.

22. An example would be the influence of these arguments, reframed by C. S. Lewis in *Mere Christianity*, on Watergate "hatchet man" Chuck Colson. Charles W. Colson, *Born Again* (Old Tappan, N.J.: Chosen, 1976), p. 119-130.

23. At this writing, six years later, we now have taken the

convocations to more than one hundred cities in ten countries of the former Soviet Union. More than forty thousand teachers and school administrators have been trained. Of these, over eighteen thousand have indicated that they received Christ. They, in turn, have shown the Jesus film and/or taught the "Christian Ethics and Morality" curriculum to at least ten million primary or secondary students and their parents in these formerly communist countries.

Chapter Three—Our God: Who He Is

1. The early church saw this as being mandated by Jesus in the Great Commission of Matthew 28:19.
2. See Charles C. Ryrie, *Basic Theology* (Wheaton, Ill.: Victor, 1987), p. 56.
3. In fact, with Tertullian, the pendulum swung too far. He saw the Son as subordinate to the Father in a way that compromised the unity of the Godhead. See L. Berkhof, *Systematic Theology* (Grand Rapids, Mich.: Eerdmans, 1939), p. 82.
4. I'm not saying we should never use analogies to illustrate the Trinity. The real value of analogies is that they make a foreign and forbidding idea (as the Trinity is for nonbelievers and to many Christians) seem less strange. I usually say something like "There are many things with which we are all familiar that are, in some ways, both three and one at the same time." These analogies do not really *explain* the Trinity. Rather, they can serve to make us less uncomfortable with the doctrine.
5. Matthew 3:16-17.
6. 1 Corinthians 8:4; see also Galatians 4:8 and James 2:19.
7. Wayne Grudem, *Systematic Theology* (Grand Rapids, Mich.: Zondervan, 1994), p. 226.
8. Monotheistic religions include Judaism, Islam, Sikhism, and the Jehovah's Witnesses (The Watchtower Society). Even the Greek philosophers Plato and Aristotle taught that there is only one true God.
9. This is also the polytheistic conception of god in Mormonism.
10. See Berkhof, *Systematic Theology,* pp. 52-81, and Grudem, *Systematic Theology,* pp. 156-225.
11. Other theologians have preferred to classify God's attributes in moral-nonmoral or absolute-relative categories. Ryrie, *Basic Theology,* 36. Erickson prefers "greatness and goodness." Millard J. Erickson, *Christian Theology* (Grand Rapids, Mich.: Baker, 1983-1985), pp. 263-300.
12. Francis A. Schaeffer, *The God Who Is There* (Chicago: InterVarsity, 1968), p. 94.

13. Process theologians assert that Greek philosophical ideas polluted early Christianity and moved it away from the dynamic, relational understanding of God that comes through in the Old Testament. This is a serious charge, so I will attempt to take my definitions not from preestablished philosophical or medieval theological categories but from the context of the Bible itself.
14. Genesis 17:1.
15. God also is called Almighty in Exodus 6:3; 2 Corinthians 6:18; Revelation 1:8,19:6; and other scriptures.
16. Some theologians classify omnipotence as a communicable attribute, presumably because other creatures can have relative degrees of power, although this justification is not explicitly made. See Grudem, *Systematic Theology*, 216-218, and Berkhof, *Systematic Theology*, pp. 79-80.
17. Malachi 3:6.
18. James 1:17.
19. Ephesians 4:30.
20. Luke 23:28; John 11:35.
21. I think this is the best way to understand verses that say God repented (Genesis 6:6 and Johah 3:10). Repentance means a change of attitude and action. When the people of Nineveh repented (Jonah 3:8-9), God changed His attitude and actions toward the city (Jonah 4:11).
22. This often is called the "free will defense" and is eloquently advocated by C. S. Lewis in *The Problem of Pain* and Alvin Plantinga in *God, Freedom, and Evil*.
23. Psalm 145:17.
24. Matthew 5:6.
25. For clinical evidence of this, see Ana-Maria Rizzuto, *The Birth of the Living God* (Chicago: University of Chicago Press, 1979).
26. I previously have written much of the story of how my own relationship with my father changed after we both came to Christ. See Alan Scholes, *The Artful Dodger: A Skeptic Confronts Christianity* (San Bernardino, Calif.: Here's Life, 1981). It is no coincidence the book is dedicated to my dad, H. M. Scholes.
27. Matthew 18:16.
28. We look more closely at the transforming power of intimate fellowship within Christ's body in chapter 13.
29. One of the best books on this subject is *Healing of Memories* by David A. Seamands (Wheaton, Ill.: Victor, 1988). See particularly chapters 7 and 8.
30. God's personal creations include both humans and angels. We will look at the personality of angels in chapter 11.

Chapter Four—Revelation: God's Various Ways of Speaking

1. I already have recounted parts of this dinner conversation in chapter 6 of *The Artful Dodger.* As in that book, for the sake of their privacy, I have changed the names of most of the people whose private conversations I have reproduced.

2. "Barth" is properly pronounced in such a way as to rhyme with "cart," the "h" being silent. The neo-orthodox revolution began with Barth's *Epistle to the Romans,* 6th ed., trans. Edwyn C. Hoskyns (New York: Oxford University, 1968). The most thorough form of Barth's theology can be found in *Church Dogmatics,* which had reached eight thousand pages but still was not complete at the time of his death in 1968.

3. This idea that the essence of Christianity is a subjective personal encounter was influenced by Søren Kierkegaard, a nineteenth-century Danish philosopher and theologian. Kierkegaard is considered "the father of existentialism," a philosophy that emphasized individual, subjective experience over objective facts. Twentieth-century neo-orthodox and existential theologians include Barth, Emil Brunner, Rudolf Bultmann, and Paul Tillich.

4. I am using the word "subjective" to mean "restricted to the experience of an individual—not publicly accessible." By "objective" I mean "external to the individual—accessible to anyone." When I say the Bible is propositional revelation and therefore objective, I mean that we all can read the same words and therefore have an objective (external) starting point for a discussion of meaning and truth. However, if revelation is only subjective (internal to each individual), then I have no clear way of knowing if someone else's experience is the same as mine—no objective reference point. The danger of the existential, neo-orthodox concept of revelation is that it leaves meaning and truth entirely subjective and relative to each individual's experience.

5. A new challenge to the evangelical idea of propositional revelation is emerging from some evangelical thinkers who are trying to formulate a "postmodern" Christianity. Most forms of postmodernism draw on the work of philosopher Ludwig Wittgenstein, who modified the existentialism of Kierkegaard. Wittgenstein adapted existentialism by saying that truth is not individualistic but rather is established and passed on by the "language games" of a community.

   Two evangelical thinkers who are trying to develop a postmodern Christianity are Nancy Murphy, *Anglo-American Postmodernity* (Boulder, Colo.: Westview, 1997) and Stanley

Grenz, *A Primer on Postmodernism* (Grand Rapids, Mich.: Eerd-mans, 1996). Both want to reject rationalism (which they see as a negative influence of the Enlightenment that has invaded the church) and with it the idea of propositional, inerrant revelation in the Bible. The basic problem I see with this view is that the Christian community, not God directly through His Word, estab-lishes what is true. The question is, which Christian community? Traditional Catholics, Mormons, Jehovah's Wit-nesses, and process-theology Methodists all claim to be the legitimate heirs of first-century Christianity. However, their ideas of truth vary wildly. In the end, I'm afraid, postmodern Chris-tianity will end up just as subjective and relative as the existential Christianity from which it was derived. See Millard Erickson's thoughtful treatment, *Postmodernizing the Faith: Evangelical Responses to the Challenge of Postmodernism* (Grand Rapids, Mich.: Baker, 1998).
6. Psalm 19:1-4.
7. Daniel 2:37-39; Romans 8:28; 13:1.
8. Romans 2:1-3,14-15.
9. Romans 1:20.
10. Genesis 31:11-13.
11. Luke 2:9-14.
12. Zechariah 1:1.
13. Hebrews 1:2-3.
14. John 14:9.
15. Matthew 24.
16. John 20:30-31.
17. General revelation can portray the creative power of God, but it takes special revelation to reveal the corrective power of God.

Chapter Five — The Bible: God's Special Way of Speaking
1. 2 Timothy 3:16.
2. 2 Peter 1:21.
3. 1 Peter 1:11.
4. Acts 28:25.
5. Mark 7:9-10.
6. Matthew 15:4.
7. Further evidence against the dictation theory comes from Luke 1:1-4. Luke said it seemed good to him, "having investigated everything carefully from the beginning, to write it out for you in consecutive order" (verse 3). If every word of Scripture was dictated by the Holy Spirit, why would Luke need to do any research? Of course, there are a few verses of Scripture that were dictated by God, such as the Ten Commandments.

8. Isaiah 55:11.
9. Warfield did defend against the claim of liberal biblical critics that there are "errors of fact or contradictions of statement" in the biblical text. For Warfield, this was simply one aspect of demonstrating that the Bible is infallible. Being error-free, for Warfield, was simply a facet of being infallible; the Bible could not have errors and still be infallible. See Benjamin Breckinridge Warfield, *The Inspiration and Authority of the Bible* (Philadelphia: Presbyterian and Reformed, 1964), pp. 423, 434-441.
10. In this chapter, I am using the Fuller faculty as the primary example of this view. However, the inerrancy controversy was widely discussed during the 1970s and 1980s in many evangelical seminaries and a number of conservative denominations, including the Southern Baptist Conference and the Missouri Synod Lutheran Church.
11. John 10:35.
12. Matthew 5:18.
13. Matthew 22:32.
14. Matthew 12:40; see also Jonah 1:17.
15. There are several possible resolutions to this problem. The simplest is the suggestion that Jesus actually was crucified and died on Thursday. The Bible nowhere states that He died on Friday. It only says He was killed before the beginning of the Sabbath. Most scholars have assumed that this was a reference to the weekly Sabbath, which begins at sundown every Friday night. However, the term "Sabbath" also was used of various other Jewish holy days. It may be that there was one of these which fell on Thursday of that particular week.
16. Charles C. Ryrie, *A Survey of Bible Doctrine* (Chicago: Moody, 1972), 40.
17. Matthew 7:29.
18. Acts 4:13.
19. Ephesians 4:14.
20. While I would view inerrancy as a logical derivative of authority, I class inerrancy as a persuasion-level belief. The current faculty at Fuller still affirm (yearly in signing the new statement of faith) the critical historic doctrines of the faith (such as the deity of Christ, salvation by grace through faith, the Virgin Birth, the bodily return of Christ, and so on). Although I think rejecting inerrancy while retaining the authority of Scripture is inconsistent and dangerous, I do not believe this is, by itself, an issue that warrants breaking fellowship. These teachers are still evangelical brothers and sisters in the faith. I, however, am glad that my own institutions (Campus Crusade for Christ and the

International School of Theology) include inerrancy in their statements of faith and I, for one, would fight to retain that clause.

21. The term "canon" literally means "measuring rod" and is used in the sense of the books that measure up to the high standard of being Scripture.

22. Wayne Grudem, *Systematic Theology*, 56-57.

23. René Pache, *The Inspiration and Authority of Scripture* (Chicago: Moody, 1969), pp. 718-179.

24. The technical terms for these writings are "Apocrypha" and "Pseudepigrapha," with the former referring to books not included in the Old Testament canon and the latter to false writings excluded from the New Testament. The adjective "apocryphal" is frequently used of any false writing, including noncanonical writings of the first through third centuries.

25. Textual scholars estimate that less than five percent of the Old Testament is open to any question as to its accuracy. For the New Testament, the questionable portion is less than one percent.

26. See Josh McDowell, *Evidence That Demands a Verdict* (San Bernardino, Calif.: Campus Crusade for Christ, 1972), pp. 43-68; René Pache, *Inspiration and Authority*, 186-198; and my own brief discussion in *Artful Dodger*, pp. 73-74.

27. Other copies of various portions of the New Testament are even earlier, including a fragment of John (the John Rylands manuscript) that dates from the early second century, less than fifty years after the Gospel was written.

28. 1 Peter 2:2.

Chapter Six—Christ: The Man Who Is God

1. My favorite musical interpretation of Jesus never reached the big screen. *The Cotton Patch Gospel*, a 1987 off-broadway stage production, renders a refreshing look at the Lord, largely through the alternately funny and moving songs by Harry Chapin and script by star Tom Key. Available on video from MDM Productions.

2. Johannes Climacus [Søren Kierkegaard], *Philosophical Fragments* or *A Fragment of Philosophy*, trans. David F. Swenson; rev. trans. by Howard V. Hong (Princeton, N.J.: Princeton University Press, 1962), pp. 49, 118-119.

3. "Propositional" truth, as we discussed in chapter 4, means that we believe God has communicated to us not only feelings or symbols but also statements that are objectively true. (A proposition is any statement about which it is meaningful to ask, "Is the statement true or false?")

4. Matthew 22:37.
5. John 16:12.
6. This is undoubtedly true until we die and have all of the effects of sin finally removed from our minds and hearts. It is my opinion that this also will be true in the eternal state. I think one of the joys of eternity will be that we forever will be learning more of the majesty, beauty, and immensity of our Creator and all He has made.
7. Schleiermacher (1768–1834) is considered the father of liberal theology.
8. Inspired by the earlier work of deist H. S. Reimarus, influential contributions to this "search" included David Strauss, *Life of Jesus, Critically Examined* (1835–1836); Ernest Renan, *Life of Jesus* (1863); Martin Kähler, *The So-Called Historical Jesus and the Historic Biblical Christ* (1892); Adolf Harnack, *What Is Christianity?* (1901); Albert Schweitzer, *The Quest of the Historical Jesus* (1906); Ernst Kasemann's article "Problem of the Historical Jesus" (1954); and Rudolf Bultmann, *Jesus and the Word* (1962).
9. During one recent Easter week, both *Time* and *U. S. News* carried cover stories that prominently featured Funk and the Jesus Seminar. *Time,* April 8, 1996, p. 52-59; *U. S. News and World Report,* April 8, 1996, p. 46-53.
10. This collection of 120 sayings attributed to Jesus was discovered in 1945 at Nag Hammadi in Egypt. Undoubtedly the church councils were aware of this collection and rejected it because (1) it was not written by the apostle Thomas, and (2) it contains teachings that are clearly Gnostic (heretical).
11. Robert W. Funk, Roy W. Hoover, and the Jesus Seminar, *The Five Gospels: The Search for the Authentic Words of Jesus* (New York: Macmillan, 1993), p. 36.
12. The miracles in John and Jesus' clear claims to divinity ran quite counter to the seminar's anti-supernatural assumptions.
13. Mark 12:17: "Render to Caesar the things that are Caesar's, and to God the things that are God's."
14. Mark 8:35.
15. Matthew 7:19.
16. John 3:7.
17. John 3:16.
18. John 4:24.
19. John 6:35.
20. John 8:7. Although the Jesus Seminar scholars agreed that this was not an authentic saying of Jesus, they nevertheless assigned the woman caught in adultery "words and story to a special

category of things they wish Jesus had said and done." Funk, et al., *Five Gospels,* p. 426.
21. John 8:32.
22. John 15:5.
23. John 15:12.
24. John 19:28,30.
25. In the introduction to *The Five Gospels,* the Jesus Seminar writers take particular aim at those of us who believe the Gospels to be inerrant (or even inspired). Strangely, their arguments are weak and unoriginal. Essentially their objections to the doctrine of inerrancy boil down to two rhetorical questions: (1) if the Bible is inerrant, why don't all present-day interpreters agree with each other; and (2) why don't we have original autographs? Although these seem like silly objections, I will briefly respond.

What gives these scholars the insight to be certain that God, having inspired the Gospels, also would be obligated to preserve all the original manuscripts and then force every subsequent reader into perfect understanding and agreement? Although it is obvious God did not do the two latter things, it is not at all obvious that He, therefore, could not have inspired the Bible. The Scriptures invite belief—they do not compel it. In Matthew 13:13-15, Jesus explained that He taught in parables so that only those with open hearts and minds would understand what He was saying. (Predictably, the Jesus Seminar puts all of this in black!) God does not force Himself (or His interpretation) on us. He invites us to follow Him, love Him, and keep His commandments. Then we will understand—John 21:19-25.

As to the second objection, I think God was wise in not allowing the original autographs to survive. He wants us to hear His Word and obey it, not worship it. If we had the original manuscripts (or anything old enough that it could possibly be an original), I'm afraid people would set up shrines and worship the paper.
26. John 5:18; 10:30.
27. John 10:36; see also Matthew 26:63-64.
28. Mark 2:5-12.
29. John 5:27.
30. John 15:26.
31. John 5:25.
32. John 20:30.
33. John 11:43-44. For a more detailed discussion of Jesus' claims of deity, see Scholes, *Artful Dodger*, pp. 29-39.
34. The Gnostics taught that matter was intrinsically evil, so that if

God showed Himself in human form, He must have only seemed to be human.

35. John 19:28.

36. Matthew 4:2.

37. John 11:35.

38. John 4:6.

39. Matthew 26:38.

40. Luke 23:46. Whether you believe human beings are bipartite (made up of body and soul only) or tripartite (composed of body, soul, and spirit), the point I wish to make is that Jesus possessed the immaterial dimension common to other humans. For an excellent argument that Jesus' nonphysical dimension was human, not solely divine, see Erickson, *Christian Theology*, pp. 708-709.

41. I hold both Jesus' humanity and His deity at the conviction level of belief. If He was not fully God or not fully man, He would not qualify to be our Savior.

42. John 1:18.

43. 1 Peter 2:21.

44. Hebrews 10:10.

45. Other biblical reasons for the Incarnation include fulfilling Old Testament prophecy (Matthew 2:6; 27:34-35), destroying the work of Satan (1 John 3:8), and becoming our High Priest to intercede with the Father on our behalf (Hebrews 5:1-10).

46. I hold the doctrine of the Virgin Birth at a strong persuasion level. While I think it is possible to be a true Christian (genuinely saved) without believing in the Virgin Birth, it is a historic doctrine of the church and found in nearly all the creeds. Similar to the doctrine of inerrancy that I discussed in chapter 5, I believe a church or Christian institution is wise to include the Virgin Birth in its boundary statements because compromise in this doctrine often has led to a later compromise in understanding Christ's deity.

47. Luke 2:52.

48. For example, in Matthew 24:36 Jesus said that He did not know the day or hour of His own return. How could He not know, if He were exercising all the attributes of deity? But this passage and others make sense if Jesus were voluntarily not using His infinite attributes during His earthly life.

49. I am embarrassed to admit that I was unclear in stating this view in my previous book, *The Artful Dodger*. At one point I said, "Jesus gave up omnipresence, or the ability to be in all places at the same time. In the same way He gave up many of His other attributes as God" (page 37). If this were literally true,

then Jesus would have ceased to be God, because His infinite
attributes are, I think, essential aspects of deity. I should have
said there what I went on to say on the next page, "Jesus didn't
stop being God; rather He voluntarily stopped using some of
the power of His deity." The earlier statement has, I'm sorry to
say, created much confusion among students of my earlier book.
50. 1 Corinthians 15:17.
51. See Acts 2:24,32; 3:15,26; 4:10; 5:30; 10:40; 13:30,33,34,37.
This doctrine is so closely tied to Jesus' deity that I believe it
deserves to be held at the conviction level. If Jesus is not alive,
then how can He save us?
52. For an excellent treatment of the intellectual issues surrounding
the Resurrection, see Stephen T. Davis, *Risen Indeed: Making
Sense of the Resurrection* (Grand Rapids, Mich.: Eerdmans,
1993).
53. I was born shortly after World War II, which makes me part of
the leading edge of what often is called the Baby Boom generation. When I speak of the "current generation," I mean those
born in the late 1960s and since (variously called "Baby Busters,"
"Generation X," "The Thirteenth Generation," and so on).

Chapter Seven — Humanity: Good News and Bad News
1. Genesis 1:27.
2. Psalm 139:13-16.
3. I personally favor the special (six-day) creation view, but I do so
on scientific, not primarily on biblical, grounds. I do not find
the scientific case for an old earth or evolution compelling but
am willing to be convinced by further evidence when, and if, it
becomes available. Because I believe any of the views (except
atheistic evolution) can be reconciled with the biblical account,
I consider this to be a persuasion-level, not a conviction-level,
issue. For a further treatment of my own views, see *Artful
Dodger,* pp. 83-94.
4. Genesis 1:31.
5. Genesis 3:7.
6. Genesis 3:8.
7. Genesis 3:16.
8. Romans 8:20-22 indicates that all creation has suffered some
consequences of the Fall. It only will be set free from its "slavery to corruption" when human redemption is complete.
9. Jeremiah 17:9.
10. Psalm 51:5.
11. Romans 3:23. I accept the Calvinist teachings of "total
depravity" and "total inability." This does not mean there is no

such thing as relative human good. Rather, it means the Fall has left all humans totally unable to live up to God's righteous standards and therefore unable to merit salvation apart from the death of Christ.

Berkhof gives an excellent description of this view. "By ascribing total inability to the natural man we do not mean to say that it is impossible for him to do good in any sense of the word. Reformed theologians generally say that he is still able to perform: (1) natural good; (2) civil good or civil righteousness; and (3) externally religious good. It is admitted that even the unrenewed possess some virtue, revealing itself in the relations of social life, in many acts and sentiments that deserve the sincere approval and gratitude of their fellow-men, and that even meet with the approval of God to a certain extent. At the same time it is maintained that these same actions and feelings, when considered in relation to God, are radically defective. Their fatal defect is that they are not prompted by love to God, or for the will of God as requiring them. When we speak of man's corruption as total inability, we mean two things: (1) that the unrenewed sinner cannot do any act, however insignificant, which fundamentally meets with God's approval and answers to the demands of God's holy law; and (2) that he cannot change his fundamental preference for sin and self to love for God, nor even make an approach to such a change." Berkhof, *Systematic Theology*, p. 247.

Chapter Eight—Salvation: God's Answer to Our Need

1. God also made other choices that can be called "election" but which will not be considered in this chapter. For example, the Bible identifies the nation of Israel as elect or chosen (Deuteronomy 4:37) and uses the same term of the coming Messiah (Isaiah 42:1).
2. Ryrie, *Survey*, p. 116.
3. The denominations strongly influenced by John Calvin (1509–1564) include Presbyterian and the various Reformed churches (Christian Reformed Church, Reformed Church in America, and so forth).
4. Arminianism is named for Jacob Arminius (1560–1609), a Dutch theologian who dissented from the Calvinism he was taught by Calvin's successor, Theodore Beza (1519–1605). Wesleyans take their name from John Wesley (1703–1791), the founder of Methodism. Wesley was converted under the influence of German Moravians, who were Arminian in their theology, and Wesley adopted many Arminian ideas into his own teaching. Modern groups with predominantly Wesleyan or

Arminian theology include Methodist, Wesleyan, and Nazarene churches and many Pentecostal and charismatic groups such as the Assemblies of God and Calvary Chapel.

5. Other verses cited by Arminians include Romans 2:4; 2 Corinthians 6:1-2.

6. Romans 8:29-30; Acts 13:48; Ephesians 1:4-5; 2 Thessalonians 2:13; Revelation 13:8; 17:8.

7. Genesis 4:6-7.

8. Ezekiel 18:32; Joel 2:12-13; Matthew 18:3-4; John 14:1; Acts 3:19; 16:31; 1 John 3:23.

9. Some Reformed theologians accuse evangelicals like me of being "Semi-Pelagian." Pelagius was a British monk who opposed Augustine's teaching that we all fell in Adam and are therefore born with a sin nature. Pelagius taught that each person is born morally free and able not to sin. His views were properly condemned by the church (at the Council of Carthage in 418). The term "Semi-Pelagian" usually refers to the traditional Roman Catholic view of original sin. In this view, all humans are affected by Adam's fall but still retain the inherent ability to cooperate with God's grace.

Reformed writer R. C. Sproul writes disparagingly of evangelicals who think there is any trace of human will left that is capable of playing even the tiniest role in salvation. "[Among evangelicals] the will is acknowledged to be severely weakened even to the point of being '99 percent' dependent upon grace for its liberation. But that one percent of unaffected moral ability or spiritual power which becomes the decisive difference between salvation and perdition is the link that preserves the chain to Pelagius. We have not broken free from the Pelagian captivity of the church." (R. C. Sproul, "Augustine and Pelagius" *TableTalk* website: www.gospelcom.net/HyperNews/get/tt/ttsubrc-06-96.html).

However, Sproul's charge of Semi-Pelagianism fails to describe my view on two counts. I am not Semi-Pelagian in the traditional Catholic mold, nor do I even hold the "one percent" view that Sproul is criticizing. I accept the Calvinist doctrine of total depravity. As a result of the Fall, we are all born completely incapable of living a righteous life, earning salvation, or even desiring a relationship with God (Romans 3:10-12). Therefore, not only do I deny the Roman Catholic form of Semi-Pelagianism, but I do not believe we are born with even "one percent of unaffected moral ability or spiritual power" that could be used to respond to God's grace. Rather, I believe that God the Holy Spirit, as a fruit of Christ's death, gives us the free gift of faith

(Ephesians 2:8-9) and restores sufficient free will that we may choose Christ.

Oddly, Sproul's complaint does not even apply to some evangelicals who are more Arminian-leaning than I. For example Thiessen, who does see election as based on foreknowledge, puts it like this: "Since mankind is hopelessly dead in trespasses and sins and can do nothing to obtain salvation, God graciously restores to all men sufficient ability to make a choice in the matter of submission to Him." Henry C. Thiessen, *Introductory Lectures in Systematic Theology* (Grand Rapids, Mich.: Eerdmans, 1949), p. 344-345.

10. I don't know any theologian who has proposed that God has predestined some to damnation (some switches off) but allows the elect to refuse salvation if they want (they can turn their own switch off or on). This view would fit my student's analogy, but I'm not aware of any theologian who holds such a view.
11. C. S. Lewis, *Miracles, A Preliminary Study* (New York: Macmillan, 1947), p. 185 footnote.
12. My view that God's sovereign choice and human free will both play a role in salvation is called "compatibilism" or "congruism." I think God's choice and our choice are compatible or congruent with each other. My view is similar to Erickson, *Christian Theology*, pp. 356-360.
13. I said in the first chapter that conviction-level beliefs are those that are "crucial to salvation." That does not mean that every doctrine we would class under salvation is equally important or that all merit classification as convictions.
14. Some translators substitute phrases for difficult words. For example, in Romans 3:25, the *New International Version* replaces "propitiation" with "sacrifice of atonement," which does not seem to me to be any clearer than the traditional choice made by the *King James Version* and the *New American Standard Bible*.
15. Hebrews 2:17.
16. 2 Corinthians 5:21.
17. 2 Corinthians 5:18-19.
18. 2 Corinthians 5:19-20.
19. Ephesians 2:8.
20. Ephesians 2:9.
21. "Faith means confidence, trust, to hold something as true. Of course, faith must have content; there must be confidence or trust about something. To have faith in Christ unto salvation means to have confidence that He can remove the guilt of sin and grant eternal life." Ryrie, *Basic Theology*, p. 326.
22. Hodges stated, "Though genuine repentance may precede

salvation (as we shall see), it need not do so. And because it is not essential to the saving transaction as such, it is in no sense a condition for that transaction." Zane C. Hodges, *Absolutely Free!* (Dallas, Tex.: Redencion Viva, 1989), p. 27.

23. "No promise of salvation is ever extended to those who refuse to accede to Christ's lordship. Thus there is no salvation except 'lordship' salvation." John MacArthur, Jr., *The Gospel According to Jesus* (Grand Rapids, Mich.: Zondervan/Academie, 1988), p. 28.

24. "Repentance is a critical element of saving faith. . . . In the sense Jesus used it, repentance calls for a repudiation of the old life and a turning to God for salvation." MacArthur, *Gospel*, p. 162.

25. "No evangelism that omits the message of repentance can properly be called the gospel, for sinners cannot come to Jesus Christ apart from a radical change of heart, mind and will. That demands a spiritual crisis leading to a complete turnaround and ultimately a wholesale transformation. It is the only kind of conversion Scripture recognizes." MacArthur, *Gospel*, p. 167.

26. This phrase is common in evangelical circles, but I have not been able to trace the quote to a specific origin. Some have suggested that Robert Munger coined it, but I have not found it in any of his published works.

27. Ephesians 2:8.

Chapter Nine—The Holy Spirit: Our Indwelling Comforter

1. Only relatively recently have systematic theologies devoted entire, separate sections to the doctrine of the Holy Spirit.

2. Romans 8:27.

3. Ephesians 4:30.

4. 1 Corinthians 12:11.

5. Psalm 139:7.

6. 1 Corinthians 2:11-12.

7. Hebrews 9:14.

8. Psalm 104:30.

9. Luke 1:35.

10. The Holy Spirit descended on the disciples with the sound of wind and tongues of fire at the Feast of Pentecost (a Jewish harvest celebration). On that occasion, all the disciples were filled with the Spirit and spoke in unlearned tongues (Acts 2:1-4).

11. Zechariah 7:12.

12. Numbers 11:29; 1 Samuel 10:10; 19:20.

13. Undoubtedly many genuine prophecies were never recorded in Scripture.

14. John 14:17. The change to a full, New Testament relationship

with the Spirit did not come until Pentecost. So as far as the Holy Spirit was concerned, these disciples were still Old Testament saints.

15. Exodus 31:3.
16. Deuteronomy 34:9.
17. Micah 3:8.
18. Luke 4:18.
19. Luke 4:1.
20. Matthew 12:28.
21. John 16:8.
22. For those who do not respond with saving faith, this rejected aspect of the gospel becomes part of the basis for God's ultimate, righteous judgment of them (John 3:19; Romans 1:18-19). Reformed theologians view this ministry of the Spirit as a part of an "external calling" that does not lead to salvation. See Berkhof, *Systematic Theology*, p. 459. I am not trying to take sides in the Calvinist-Arminian debate over whether faith comes before or after regeneration. My only point is that this convicting ministry of the Spirit is to all people, whether they eventually respond and are saved or not. Christian thinkers have long debated whether saving faith logically precedes regeneration (the Arminian position) or regeneration precedes faith (the Calvinist position). For discussions on each side, see Erickson, *Christian Theology*, pp. 932-933, and Berkhof, *Systematic Theology*, pp. 471-472, 490-492.
23. Titus 3:5.
24. 2 Corinthians 5:17.
25. See previous note (number 22) on the issue of whether regeneration precedes faith.
26. In Romans 8:9 and 1 Corinthians 3:16, Paul said that if we are believers, then the Spirit of God "dwells in" us. The Greek word for "dwell" means "to take up residence." In 1 Corinthians 7:12-13, Paul used the same Greek word to refer to a husband and wife living together. When the Holy Spirit indwells us, He not only comes to live within us, but He begins an intimate, personal relationship with us.
27. Because of his disobedience, King Saul lost the Holy Spirit and was indwelt instead by an evil spirit (1 Samuel 16:14). Having seen this, David prayed, "Do not take Thy Holy Spirit from me" (Psalm 51:11). Believers do not need to pray this prayer today.
28. 1 Corinthians 3:3.
29. 1 Corinthians 6:15.
30. 1 Corinthians 6:16-19. See also Ephesians 4:30.
31. The basic problem with the Pentecostal theology of baptism is

that it is largely based on the book of Acts. It is dangerous to base doctrine for today solely or primarily on a historical book of the Bible. This is because historical books describe God's dealings with particular people at specific times. A better way to understand tongues and Spirit baptism in Acts is to recognize that this was a transitional period between how the Holy Spirit related to Old Testament believers (including those in the time of the Gospels) and how He would now relate to post-Pentecost believers. The best way to establish doctrine is to look at the New Testament Epistles, especially those of Paul, which were specifically designed to teach normative doctrine for the church age. Despite the Corinthian believers' carnality, Paul seemed confident that all those in the Corinthian church were baptized into one body and made to drink of the Holy Spirit (1 Corinthians 12:13). He could not be confident of this if the baptism of the Spirit were a second event in the Christian life. In fact, if the baptism were a later experience that led to spiritual power, Paul would have had good reason to question whether any of the Corinthians had it.

While I disagree with the Pentecostal understanding of Spirit baptism, I believe this is a persuasion-level, not a conviction-level, issue. Most Pentecostals and charismatics hold an orthodox view of the Trinity, including the full deity and personality of the Holy Spirit. Because we agree on the crucial conviction-level teaching regarding the Spirit, I fellowship with them as brothers and sisters in Christ.

32. Ephesians 4:30.
33. See also 2 Corinthians 1:22; Ephesians 1:13.
34. John 16:12-15. I am interpreting these verses to be a prediction by Jesus of an ongoing ministry to all post-Pentecost believers. This is the view of a number of evangelical theologians, including Erickson, *Christian Theology*, p. 874, and Ryrie, *Basic Theology*, p. 380. Others see these verses as a prediction of the coming further revelation of the New Testament canon. See Lewis and Demarest, *Integrative Theology*, I:144-145. (Zondervan, 1987).
35. Evangelical theologians refer to this ministry as "illumination." While existential and neo-orthodox theologians frequently confuse illumination with revelation, evangelicals have generally made the crucial and proper distinction between revelation (the Spirit's now-completed work of inspiring the original writers of Scripture) and illumination (the Spirit's ongoing work of aiding believers to understand what He has already revealed).
36. Romans 12:7; 1 John 2:27.

37. Romans 8:14.
38. I have intentionally used the word "interdependence" instead of the more usual "dependence." God does not, of course, need us in the same way we need Him. However, He has sovereignly chosen to make us partners in His plan for the ages. We have the awesome privilege of being His agents, His royal ambassadors to a fallen world (2 Corinthians 5:20).
39. James 1:5.
40. Psalm 37:4-5.
41. 1 Kings 19:12-13.
42. Despite the fact that both have their source in the same Spirit, divine leading is not inerrant in the same way the Scriptures are. The difference is that God did a unique work of inspiration in superintending the Bible to prevent any human error from creeping in. However, it is quite possible for us to misunderstand the Spirit's subjective leading. Our enemies—the world, the Devil, and the flesh—can and do masquerade as the voice of God. Therefore, if God's subjective leading seems to be moving us away from the counsel of His Word, we must trust His Word and doubt the supposed "subjective" leading.
43. Romans 8:26.
44. 1 Peter 4:10.
45. Acts 1:8. All of these various ministries of the Spirit, while clearly taught in the Bible, need not be understood for one to be saved. So I would class all of these teachings at the persuasion level.

Chapter Ten—Christian Growth: Our Walk of Faith
1. 1 Peter 1:16 (KJV).
2. 1 Corinthians 6:11.
3. 2 Corinthians 5:17.
4. Other verses that speak of sanctification in the past tense include Acts 20:32 and 26:18. The word "saint" comes from the same root as sanctification and holy. That is why the New Testament frequently uses the word "saint" to refer to anyone who is a believer and therefore has received positional sanctification (Acts 9:13,32; 26:10; Romans 1:7; 8:27; 1 Corinthians 1:2; 2 Corinthians 1:1; Ephesians 1:1; 6:18; Philippians 1:1).
5. 1 Thessalonians 5:23.
6. This includes the negative aspect of moral purity, being free from sin, but also includes all the positive aspects of Christlike character such as love, joy, peace, patience, and so on (Galatians 5:22-23).
7. See also 1 John 4:16-19.

8. 1 John 1:8. Many Methodists, Wesleyans, and Nazarenes, following the teachings of John Wesley, believe that something they call "utter sanctification" is possible in this earthly life. However, neither Wesley nor his followers viewed this as complete conformity to Christ in thought, word, and deed. They teach, rather, that some believers reach the point where they never again intentionally sin. However, even these saints who have reached utter sanctification still can sin inadvertently through sins of omission, immaturity, and so forth. See Melvin E. Dieter, "The Wesleyan Perspective," *Five Views on Sanctification* (Grand Rapids, Mich.: Zondervan, 1987), p. 13-14. Interestingly, John Wesley himself never claimed to have reached this stage of utter sanctification.

9. Colossians 1:22.

10. 1 Corinthians 15:51,52.

11. I used to think life in heaven would be a kind of static perfection. Now I believe there will be exciting and challenging growth, discovery, and accomplishment in the eternal state. Complete holiness means I will be separated from sin and temptation and truly free for the first time to use all my talent, creativity, and energy in the ways they were always meant to be used.

12. 1 Samuel 13:14; see also Acts 13:22.

13. Galatians 3:2-3.

14. Ephesians 4:30.

15. This view of the ministry of the Spirit is actually just a clarification and simplification of Keswick and dispensational teachings that were first popularized more than a hundred years ago in England. One current proponent of this view is Bill Bright and the ministry of Campus Crusade for Christ. This teaching is also consistent with the views of a number of Reformed thinkers. See J. Robertson McQuilkin, "The Keswick Perspective," *Five Views*, pp. 151-183. Also see Anthony A. Hoekema, "Response to McQuilkin," *Five Views*, p. 187.

16. Hebrews 12:15.

17. 1 John 1:9.

18. The analogy of breathing is an apt one because the Greek word *pneuma* can mean either "spirit" or "breath."

19. I do not believe that anything covered in this chapter should be classed as a conviction. Because the entire doctrine of sanctification deals with what happens after a person receives Christ, all of these teachings are either persuasion- or opinion-level beliefs.

Chapter Eleven — The Invisible War: Our Supernatural Allies and Enemies

1. It is difficult for a Christian to weigh the authenticity of these reports. Some of the accounts sound very much like biblical angels; others have more of a new age flavor.
2. A notable exception is the popular television show "Touched by an Angel," which seems much closer to the Bible in its portrayal of God's angels.
3. Nehemiah 9:6; Colossians 1:16.
4. Because none of the teachings in this chapter are directly connected to salvation, I do not hold anything about angels at the conviction level. Most of the ideas I explore here are based directly on biblical revelation and so may be viewed as persuasions. A few, however, are speculative questions, such as whether every person has a single guardian angel. These issues on which the Scripture is silent (or nearly so) are best treated as tentative opinions.
5. 1 Peter 1:12.
6. Luke 2:13.
7. Jude 6.
8. Isaiah 6:2; Ezekiel 1:5-11. The "angel of the LORD" in the Old Testament is probably an appearance of Christ in a human body before His incarnation (what theologians call a "theophany" or a "Christophany"). See Genesis 16:7-13; 21:11-18; Judges 2:1-4; 6:11-24; 13:2-22.
9. Hebrews 1:13-14.
10. 1 Corinthians 14:33.
11. Jude 9.
12. Daniel 10:13. "Prince" is a term often used of angels, both good and evil.
13. Genesis 3:24.
14. Isaiah 6:2.
15. It may be that "archangel" is a third type of angel or that it is simply a designation of a role. For example, Michael may be a cherub (a type of angel) and an archangel (his leadership role).
16. Revelation 5:11.
17. Isaiah 6:3; Hebrews 1:6; Revelation 5:11-13.
18. Revelation 21:9; 22:9.
19. Job 38:4-7.
20. Daniel 12:1.
21. Daniel 10:20-21.
22. Revelation 9:13-18; 16:1-12.
23. Acts 12:21-23.
24. Luke 2:13.

25. Matthew 2:13.
26. Matthew 4:11.
27. Matthew 26:53.
28. Luke 22:43.
29. Matthew 28:2.
30. Hebrews 1:14.
31. Acts 12:5-11.
32. Acts 27:21-26.
33. Many Bible scholars feel Matthew 18:10 teaches that every child has a specific angel. If so, then presumably angels watch over all children, not only those of believers.
34. 1 Kings 19:12 (KJV).
35. A good example of this is the way Peter gave God credit for his escape from prison (Acts 12:17), although God had used an angel to accomplish the miracle (Acts 12:7-10).
36. Job 1:9-10.
37. Author's update: The dizziness did continue for nearly three months, but I am now free from all effects of the accident.
38. Why did God choose to remove the angelic hedge enough to allow me to get hit at all? The larger answer is the one I gave in chapter 3. God can bring greater good from a world of free moral agents that also contains evil than from a "perfect" world where no evil (and no real freedom) is allowed. But why did this particular bad thing happen to me at this time? At least a part of the answer is that, while destruction and pain are not good things in themselves, God can use them for good (Romans 8:28) to teach me greater dependence, patience, and compassion for others in pain.
39. The meetings at the Forum were part of the "Berkeley Blitz," a week-long outreach sponsored by Campus Crusade for Christ. The week ended with Billy Graham preaching to an overflow audience in the Berkeley Greek Theater.
40. At that time in Berkeley, particularly on Telegraph Avenue, it was usual for people my age to wear beards, beads, flowers in their hair, ear and nose rings, and clothing in garish psychedelic colors. Street music and spontaneous oriental-style dancing were also common.
41. I learned later that Lambert was alluding to Matthew 12:22-29. The Pharisees had accused Jesus of casting out demons by the power of Satan. The Lord proved their idea foolish and asserted that His power comes from the Holy Spirit (verse 28). He then explained what He was doing by analogy. The world is Satan's "house" or stronghold. Jesus was invading Satan's territory and, in order to do so, He first had to bind Satan (the strong man).

We do not have the power to bind Satan or his demons, but Jesus did and still does. So Lambert's prayer that God would deny Satan's access to the room through the blood of Christ was appropriate (and effective). See also the parallel account in Mark 3:21-27.

42. Lambert is a physicist and at that time worked for Stanford Research Institute.
43. Matthew 13:39; Luke 10:18; 11:18.
44. Matthew 4:1-11.
45. Isaiah 14:12 (KJV).
46. Ephesians 6:11-12; Ezekiel 28:14.
47. In Ezekiel 28:12, God says to him, "You had the seal of perfection, full of wisdom and perfect in beauty." There is a problem with this view if "archangel" is one type of angel and "cherub" is another. In that case Lucifer as a cherub was created lower than Michael, who is called an archangel. However, if archangel is a role or position, then Lucifer may have originally held a position equal to, or even greater than, Michael.
48. 2 Corinthians 4:4.
49. Ephesians 2:2.
50. 2 Corinthians 11:3.
51. Revelation 12:17.
52. 2 Timothy 2:26.
53. Job 1:6-12.
54. Ezekiel 28:14.
55. Isaiah 14:13-14.
56. Matthew 4:9.
57. 2 Corinthians 4:4.
58. Luke 8:12.
59. Acts 5:3.
60. 1 Corinthians 7:5.
61. Matthew 12:24.
62. "Stars" is one of several terms used for angels in the Old Testament (Isaiah 14:13; Daniel 8:10).
63. 1 Timothy 4:1-3.
64. Matthew 8:28-32.
65. Matthew 12:24.
66. Daniel 10:12-13.
67. Revelation 16:14.
68. Matthew 9:33; Luke 13:11.
69. Matthew 25:41.
70. 1 John 4:4.
71. James 4:7.
72. Ephesians 2:1-3.

73. 1 John 2:15.
74. Romans 12:2.
75. James 4:7.
76. Romans 13:14.
77. 2 Timothy 2:22.
78. 2 Corinthians 4:4; 2 Peter 1:4; 1 John 2:16.
79. Matthew 4:3-9; 1 John 5:19.
80. John 17:18-19.
81. Genesis 39:6-12.
82. 1 Timothy 4:1; Revelation 2:24. I think Satan himself is quite pleased with the Faustus legend (especially its American versions, "The Devil and Daniel Webster," and "Damn Yankees"), which promotes the notion that a clever person could outsmart the Devil.
83. Matthew 4:1-11.
84. 1 Peter 5:8.
85. Estimates vary, but most scholars date the beginning of post-modernism in the United States to the late 1960s or early 1970s.
86. Ephesians 6:12. As with the teachings on sanctification and on good angels, much in this chapter about Satan, demons, and spiritual warfare is clearly taught in Scripture. But none of it, in my view, is crucial to salvation. Therefore, I would classify these teachings as persuasions.

Chapter Twelve — The Church: Our New Family
1. W. E. Vine, *An Expository Dictionary of New Testament Words,* vol. 2 (Westwood, N.J.: Revell, 1940), p. 90.
2. 1 John 1:3.
3. 1 Corinthians 1:9.
4. 2 Corinthians 13:14.
5. John 13:34-35.
6. Psalm 34:3.
7. Isaiah 25:1 (NIV). See also Exodus 15:2; 2 Samuel 22:47; Psalm 18:46; 99:5,9; 107:32; 118:28.
8. It is called a worship "service" because one of the ways we can *serve* God is by lifting Him up in worship.
9. Isaiah 14:13-14.
10. Genesis 3:4-5.
11. In the Western world since the Enlightenment, we've placed great faith in the ability of the human mind, unaided by God or any other authority, to eventually discover all truth. Likewise, technology and "progress," we've been assured, will eventually solve all human problems. In the United States we have further

reinforced our natural sinfulness with values such as independence, freedom, autonomy, and a general mistrust of all
authority.
12. James 4:10.
13. 1 Peter 5:6.
14. Matthew 23:11-12. Jesus' incarnation followed this pattern of
humility resulting in exultation (Philippians 2:5-11).
15. Isaiah 6:1-3.
16. Revelation 5:11-12; see also Revelation 4:8-11.
17. Revelation 4:10-11; 5:13-14.
18. Ephesians 5:15-16.
19. Ephesians 5:17.
20. Ephesians 5:18-19.
21. Hebrews 12:28.
22. When I speak of God "smiling," I am of course using a
metaphor. Because God does not have a literal, physical face, He
does not literally smile (though Jesus did and does). When I
speak of God smiling at us, I mean that He experiences the
emotions of pride, pleasure, and joy—emotions that all are
ascribed to Him in the Bible.
23. Zephaniah 3:17 (NIV). See also Isaiah 62:3-5. Although these
passages are speaking prophetically of God's future joy and
delight in the restoration of Israel, the image of God taking
delight as a bridegroom is repeated in the New Testament of
Christ as the bridegroom of the church (Ephesians 5:25-27;
Revelation 19:7). Then the two images are joined in Revelation
21, where Jerusalem is called the bride of Christ (verses 9-10).
24. Quoted by Grudem, *Systematic Theology*, p. 441.
25. I have intentionally not specified a particular style or form of
worship. I find that at various times I can be aided toward an
attitude of worship by a wide variety of forms of service and
styles of music. I believe that God takes joy in any form of worship that is offered from a joyful heart. Because I do not see any
specific forms of worship commanded in the Bible, I would
class forms or styles of worship as matters of opinion.
26. 1 Thessalonians 5:11; see also 5:14.
27. John 14:16 (KJV).
28. Hebrews 3:13 (KJV); see also Titus 2:15.
29. David Augsburger, *Caring Enough to Confront,* rev. ed. (Ventura,
Calif.: Regal, 1981), p. 52.
30. Is the office of deaconess biblical? Phoebe is called a deacon
(servant) in Romans 16:1, and in the middle of Paul's discussion of deacons, Paul mentioned that women should also be
"dignified, not malicious gossips, but temperate, faithful in all

things" (1 Timothy 3:11). The words "their wives" in the *New International Version* and some other modern translations have been added. The Greek just says "women." Evangelical commentators are divided on the meaning and application of these verses. In my view these two passages taken together indicate there was at least an informal, and probably a formal, role for women deacons in the early church. The Bible is completely silent as to whether there were women who performed the role of elder. This is, in my view, a matter of persuasion.

31. 1 Timothy 3:1. The word used in this passage is "overseer," but nearly all evangelical Bible scholars view this as a reference to the same role in the church as elder.

32. Ryrie, *Survey*, p. 144.

33. My point is not that someone so gifted should not serve as the principal overseer in a church, but rather that individuals whose primary gifts are exhortation, mercy, serving, and so on, may also be good choices, providing they meet the other biblical qualifications for leadership.

34. Of course, the teaching that God is worthy of our worship is a conviction-level doctrine. I view that as a teaching that flows out of an understanding of the attributes of God (see chapter 3) rather than an aspect of the doctrine of the church.

35. Ephesians 5:25-27.

Chapter Thirteen—Last Things: When We See Him Face to Face

1. 1 Corinthians 13:12 (KJV).

2. This doesn't mean that we will know everything. In chapter 3 I classed omniscience (having all knowledge) as one of God's infinite (incommunicable) attributes. This means that none of God's creations, including all angels and humans, will ever know everything. Instead, I think Paul was speaking of an intimacy of relationship with God that exceeds anything the greatest mystic has yet experienced.

3. See 1 Corinthians 2:9.

4. This would be true of nearly all Christians who accept the Bible as a primary authoritative source of information about the future, whether Protestant, Catholic, or Orthodox.

5. Matthew 22:31-32.

6. 1 Corinthians 15:12-26.

7. Matthew 5:22; 10:28; Mark 9:43-45.

8. John 14:1-3; Colossians 1:5; 1 Peter 1:4.

9. Acts 1:11.

10. John 20:27.

11. Revelation 20:11-15.
12. 1 Corinthians 3:11-15; 2 Corinthians 5:10.
13. Revelation 12:10; 20:10.
14. Out of all of the teachings on which most Christians agree, the two most crucial, and the two which I would class as convictions, are the related doctrines that Jesus will return and that there will be a final judgment. If Jesus never returns and there is no final judgment, then there is no final solution to sin, no ultimate justice, and our salvation will never be complete. All of the other teachings in this chapter are, in my view, either persuasion- or opinion-level beliefs.
15. Revelation 20:2,3,4,5,6,7.
16. The phrase "thousand years" occurs only three other places, and none of them seems to be a direct reference to the Millennium. See Psalm 90:4, Ecclesiastes 6:6, and 2 Peter 3:8.
17. The prefix "a" means "not." This view is called "amillennial" because it holds the Millennium is not going to be a literal thousand-year period.
18. Amillennialists would argue that very few would try to take everything in Revelation literally, for example, the seals, trumpets, and bowls. See Revelation 6:1, 8:6, 21:9.
19. "Post" means "after." This view is called "postmillennial" because it holds that Christ will return after the Millennium.
20. Some postmillennialists think the period will be exactly a thousand years long, while others consider it to be simply a long period of indeterminate length.
21. "Pre" means "before." Premillennialists believe Christ will return before the Millennium.
22. While most premillennialists envision a literal thousand-year reign, some see the number as simply representing a long period.
23. Some historic premillennialists think the new heaven and earth begin at the return of Christ, before the Millennium.
24. Matthew 24:21.
25. This position also is referred to as classic or historic premillennialism and sometimes even "chiliasm" (from the Greek word *chilioi*, which means "a thousand").
26. 1 Thessalonians 4:16-17. The term "rapture" comes from the Latin *rapio*, which means "to snatch or carry away."
27. A variant of this view says that the Rapture of the church happens midway through the Tribulation, allowing believers to avoid the more violent second half. There is also a "partial rapture" theory that can be combined with either the "pre" or "mid" views. According to the partial view, only some believers

are taken (those who are spiritual or obedient).

28. I do believe that individual societies, such as eighteenth-century England under the influence of the Wesleys, have temporarily changed for the better, and it is proper and biblical for believers to strive for this sort of change in their own time and place. I do not believe that the world as a whole is, or will be, getting better. The pervasiveness of sin (even in Christians) and the widespread influence of Satan and his demons will prevent radical, permanent change from happening until Christ returns to rule.

29. Luke 18:8.

30. Galatians 3:28-29.

31. Matthew 24:36,44. See also Matthew 24:42; 25:13; Mark 13:32-37; 1 Thessalonians 5:1-4; and Revelation 3:3.

32. This is also an argument against the midtribulational view.

33. See Matthew 25:21; Luke 19:17.

34. See also Matthew 25:14-30; Luke 19:12-26.

35. This view works whether we see the crowns as literal head-pieces made of gold or as symbolic of honor, glory, and so forth. In this discussion, for simplicity, I will speak of the crowns as if they are literal.

36. 2 Timothy 4:8.

37. Other passages that speak of believers receiving crowns include James 1:12, 1 Peter 5:4, Revelation 2:10, and 3:11.

38. Revelation 4:1-11. Some have suggested this is the judgment seat of Christ and that the one on the throne is Jesus. Others say it is the throne of God the Father.

39. 1 Corinthians 3:12-15 pictures two kinds of works, those that are burned up by the testing fire (wood, hay, and straw) and those that survive (gold, silver, and precious stones). It is reasonable to interpret Paul as teaching that the works that survive testing are those done in the power of the Holy Spirit because that is the larger context of Paul's discussion in chapter 3.

40. 1 Corinthians 3:15.

41. Revelation 21:4.

42. C. S. Lewis, *The Last Battle* (New York: Macmillan, 1956), pp. 160-162.

43. John 14:1-3.

44. Likewise, whatever the horrors of the physical environment, what will make hell hellish is that the damned will be cut off forever from God and everything beautiful He has created.

INDEX OF KEY TERMS AND FIGURES

DR. ALAN KENT SCHOLES

ALAN SCHOLES has been a staff member with Campus Crusade for Christ for thirty years. During the past twenty-five years, he has spoken throughout the United States as well as in Russia, Europe, Africa, and Asia. Alan is currently teaching theology for the International School of Theology at Arrowhead Springs in Southern California. He has also taught at Talbot Theological Seminary. Alan holds three masters degrees and a Ph.D. in theology from the Claremont School of Theology. Alan is the author of numerous articles and two books. He twice has visited Russia, at the invitation of the Russian Ministry of Education, where (along with an international team of scholars and educators) he trained more than fifteen hundred Russian teachers to teach Christianity in their public school systems. Alan and his wife, Jan, live in the mountain community of Crestline, California.